Courage to Climb
12 Women Surmount the Impossible

"Not often do you discover a book that speaks to so many in such a raw and vulnerable way. Sherry Shoemaker has painstakingly taken several years of her life to commit to providing a voice of assurance for those who have a story to tell that they believe will empower other women to find their voice as well. "Courage To Climb" is a must read for all women, whether to reinforce what they already know or empower them to find the courage to climb."

— Audrey Cupo, Professional Organizer
A BETTER SPACE

"Courage to Climb is empowering, humbling, and frightening all at the same time. These stories of personal strength and perseverance resonate and encourage us all to look inside, be honest, and move forward with self-respect, confidence and love."

— Sue Kent, PharmD
Clinical Assistant Professor

"In a straightforward, conversational style Sherry portrays inspiring stories of women who overcame obstacles in their lives through courage and faith."

— Cindy Bergvall
Director at Bee, Bergvall, & Co

I

Courage to Climb

12 Women Surmount the Impossible

by **Sherry Shoemaker**

Publisher: Sherry Shoemaker

SShoemaker1@gmail.com

All names written in the chapters were given with verbal consent of the interviewee. Interviewees gave a verbal consent for free author interpretation of recorded interviews.

ISBN-10:1492122521

ISBN-13: 978-1492122524

Table of Contents

Foreword

Chapter One — Thomasine Landis.................................. 1

Chapter Two — Marirose Haffey................................... 11

Chapter Three — Darla Pompilio 21

Chapter Four — Barbara Marte 31

Chapter Five — Sharon Snyder................................... 43

Chapter Six — Tracey Dougherty................................ 53

Chapter Seven — Suzanne Richardson 63

Chapter Eight — Mary Sheila 73

Chapter Nine — Amy Stevens.................................... 83

Chapter Ten — Dawn Reider..................................... 93

Chapter Eleven — Nancy Venner 101

Chapter Twelve — Sherry Shoemaker......................... 111

Acknowledgments.. 123

Foreword

Codependency has affected my life since I was a child. Over the years, I have controlled, compromised, resented, felt guilty, schemed, manipulated, waited for the other shoe to drop, made all the contingency plans for every situation and been a pleaser. My inner negative voice has told me, "You are not good enough," or it's driven me to strive to be the perfect wife, have the perfect house, be the perfect mother and become the perfect businesswoman. I have often reveled in the knowledge that if I wanted anything, I would get it, whatever the cost to me. By the year 2004, my marriage was in shambles, and I was totally exhausted.

How does such a person write a book about empowerment?

Anyone familiar with the condition will recognize that I was struggling with codependency. (The term today refers to people who are susceptible to being affected by another person's behavior while also remaining inordinately focused on controlling that person's behavior.) I eventually found Al-Anon, learned to control what I can in my life and detach from what I can't and then I shifted my focus to let go and let God. One year later, I found myself stepping out of my comfort zone and going back to school to become a life coach.

Coaching, I discovered, was my God-given purpose, and it was why I'd experienced all the good and bad in my life. It is my mission, my career and, in some ways, my own salvation. And yet, it is not the endpoint. After all, empowerment doesn't come quickly or easily. After my training (and countless hours of introspective work), my own coach said to me, "You need to write a book." I didn't reject this idea outright, but it did take me more than two years to work up the nerve to start it. Just the thought of it made me queasy! But what spurred me on was the knowledge that, as long as I felt supported and trusted that I was doing what God meant for me to do, I could do anything. This faith would, ironically, become a motif in this book.

And the book, in some ways, began to form of its own accord. Yes, I'd lived through and learned from enough experiences to write a book twice as long as this one. But what really was astonishing was that I encountered woman after woman who, like me, had moved from a place of pain to a place of empowerment. Women who had abandoned their victim-hood for something better and more fulfilling. These women and their stories inspired me to write.

I began interviewing these women in 2011. Their stories were as different as the women themselves. Some of them had overcome abusive relationships, some had confronted unspeakable loss, some had surmounted impossible professional barriers — you name it, these women had dealt with it. I personally knew some of them, but others just came out of the woodwork, almost as if their destinies and mine were intertwined in the writing of this book. They appeared right when I most needed to speak with them. The result of their willingness to share is this collection of powerful stories you'll find in the following pages.

As I spoke with these women, a pattern began to emerge. Not only had they worked hard to make their lives better, they all shared a handful of inspiring characteristics like courage, passion, faith and strength. They all had to make critical, difficult choices in order to empower themselves to live better lives. My hope is that, after reading this book and doing the work in the Reflections sections, you may begin a shift in your life, too.

You'll find my own story within these pages, but at the end of this writing project, I realize yet another connection to the women profiled here. I had to make a difficult decision to devote the time, energy and risk inherent to such a personal book and really commit to it. Often times I wrote first thing in the morning before I started my workday. And all the numerous personal issues that arose in my life simply had to be worked around. My son's wedding, taking care of my mom throughout many medical issues and hospitalizations over the last two years, mending my own broken wrist (replete with plates and screws), addressing several serious health concerns of my 12-year-old Samoyed and dealing with the continued ups and downs of my marriage — these are just a few of the things I encountered while writing this book.

Still, I persevered. If nothing else, these women have taught me that, when you have passion, dedication and positive support, anything is possible. Even a book. May these pages inspire you as much as they have inspired me.

Many Blessings,

Sherry Shoemaker

August 2013

Chapter One:
Thomasine Landis

Until 2008, Thomasine Landis was an outgoing, attractive and fun-loving lady who, by all appearances, had the perfect life. She was 49 years old, and she loved her job. (A trained nurse, Thomasine worked her way up to become the client-services manager at a senior-assistance company.) She had a house, a dog, a husband who supported her and a 20-year-old son in college.

Behind closed doors, however, her story was anything but perfect.

Thomasine's husband, Paul, was an alcoholic. That alone was bad enough, but she'd learned to cope with it by creating a separate life for herself and her son, Jason. She routinely attended work and personal events by herself, leaving Paul alone at home to drink. She would make up excuses as to why her husband couldn't attend. Nobody seemed to question her.

But the rape by her husband was something she couldn't ignore. In September 2008, she began taking sleeping pills to quell her anxiety and help her sleep at night. One morning, however, she awoke to find herself naked in bed and alone. She figured out that Paul, while in a drunken stupor, had sex with her unresponsive body. She was terrorized and humiliated. How, she wondered, could her husband of 21 years respect her so little that he could do that? She'd loved, trusted and supported him, despite his addiction, and this was the consequence? Thomasine was embarrassed, yes, but also deeply ashamed for not stopping him, and she began to lose her own self-respect as a result. It wasn't just about the rape, though. It was everything the rape symbolized, from the cheapening of her devotion to him, to the domineering position Paul assumed in the marriage. No longer equal in their union, and no longer able to trust him, Thomasine embarked on a downward spiral of depression that led her to attempt suicide a month later.

Carefully, Thomasine calculated how to kill herself: She took 10 sleeping pills and 10 antidepressants. When these didn't work right away, she took another 10 of each. Her husband found her unconscious in bed the next morning and rushed her to the hospital. After losing three days in a coma — and two-and-a-half weeks in the hospital — Thomasine awoke feeling completely defeated. She'd failed in her marriage, and now she'd failed in her suicide. Worse, when Paul visited her, the smell of alcohol on his breath only sickened her further. Why, she wondered, wouldn't he stop drinking? Professionally, she understood alcoholism was a disease that couldn't be immediately cured any more than a cold can go away because you wish it would. But as a wife, she couldn't understand how Paul could continue to drink when the result was her lying in a hospital bed after a suicide attempt. Thomasine, who had always been there to help others, now needed help herself.

One consequence of a failed suicide attempt is that it strips the veneer off of your life. Now everyone knew that Thomasine's world was desperately unhappy. But Thomasine couldn't see a way out. Ending the marriage would, she knew, be viewed as a failure on her part by her family, who wouldn't accept a divorce. And she had to consider Jason, for whom she wanted to set the example of an enduring marriage. So she assumed the role of a good Catholic girl and clung to the illusion that Paul would eventually stop drinking and be honest with her.

Thomasine began going to therapy — alone, because Paul refused to go with her — and her depression slowly lifted. (She even joked with her doctors that it was her husband she should have tried to kill and not herself.) This struggle consumed the next two months of Thomasine's life as she went about her daily business. And things weren't all bad. Thomasine's professional life was just about to take off: She had earned the opportunity to become a partner in her business. She planned on buying into the company with money she'd inherited from her father and carefully set aside as a nest egg for her future. Finally, during the Christmas week of 2008, that future was beginning to unfold. She was content, happy even, as she went to the bank to withdraw the requisite funds. But when she made the request of the teller, her dreams evaporated. She discovered Paul had created an account with the money in his name only — not a joint account as he'd promised — and that the money was gone.

Thomasine believes people are inherently good, and that goes a long way toward explaining why an intelligent woman would entrust her money to a man who'd deceived and disappointed her throughout their marriage. She had also, quite simply, never thought Paul was capable of robbing her. Yes, she could see with hindsight that she had given Paul all the power, and that she'd done everyone — especially Jason

— a disservice by not dealing head-on with his alcoholism. The fact that she'd never questioned or even reviewed their bank accounts took on a whole new dimension at that point. It was bad enough not to know what was in them, but now it was downright destructive, both to her professional plans and to her marriage. While she sincerely wanted to make her marriage work, she had to question her own limits with regard to her self-respect and dignity.

Thomasine saw that Paul had made multiple withdrawals over the months, and she suspected he was gambling. Shocked and enraged, she confronted Paul. He stonily replied that he didn't know what happened to the money. He claimed he'd put it into an account that would get a better return, and he hadn't wanted to "bother her" with the transfer. Feeing angry, scared and heartbroken, Thomasine resolved then and there to regain her self-respect.

It was cold and snowy that night, and Thomasine wasn't wearing anything but her flannel pajamas and slippers, but she instinctively bolted for the door and drove to a friend's house. She had to get out of that toxic marriage, and it had to be then.

From the safety of her friend's home, Thomasine realized she didn't care if she ever returned home. She left behind her belongings and her adult son. She brought no money with her — there wasn't any to take even if she'd wanted to. But while she grappled with the guilt and freedom surging simultaneously through her body, she somehow knew that her life had just changed for the better. Yes, she had a lot to lose. But she knew first-hand what she was teaching her son by staying in her marriage. She'd grown up in the shadow of alcoholics and abusive relationships only to find herself in the same kind of marriage. Would Jason treat women the same way?

The only hope she had of helping him avoid that fate was to leave. But she'd survived a bitter divorce between her parents and wanted at least to spare Jason the vitriol of that experience. So while she could've pressed charges against Paul for embezzlement, fraud and rape, she didn't. Anger consumed her, but she only allowed it to guide her as far as leaving the relationship. She realized that she needed to stand up for herself and set an example by ending her marriage with dignity. That included shunning materialistic desires and concerns — she wasn't going back for her things, and she wasn't going to sue Paul for all he was worth (or wasn't worth, as the case may have been). To Thomasine, her self-respect and dignity were more important than any materialistic thing. Besides, she needed to prove to herself that she could indeed make a new life on her own.

Because Thomasine worked with the elderly, she was able to stay with a client while she filed for divorce. The distance and the momentum of moving on with her life helped her learn to forgive Paul without condoning his actions. He had a disease, and her feeling angry and resentful only gave him the power she was working hard to regain for herself. She stepped though the fear of being alone to embrace the fact that she could work and care for herself. Her life could be whole again without Paul.

Today, appearances and reality match up for Thomasine. She still has a great relationship with her son and sees him often. And she is happily remarried to someone who respects and loves her. What's more, she believes herself to be worthy of that love and respect, and so she and her husband practice full disclosure on every topic, including finances, which she oversees personally. Equally important, Thomasine has learned to surround herself with positive people who support her instead of judge or entrap her. She still loves her job, but now she loves her life at home, too.

Reflections

Thomasine's story resonates with many people, regardless of their marital experiences. Why? Because her story is about losing self-respect and ceding personal autonomy, two mistakes a lot of people make in a lot of different ways.

Today Thomasine has the courage speak up and honor her needs without feeling intimidated. She can set boundaries in her relationships both at home and in her career without feeling guilty, and she loves giving back to others in need. The reason she can do these things is because she has a solid sense of identity. As Melody Beattie describes in her book, "Beyond Codependency: And Getting Better All the Time," an identity consists of concrete, attainable goals like having good friends and a career you enjoy. It also consists of positive feelings like a sense of fulfillment, a sense of safety and believing in a higher power.

As you continue in your own personal development, consider these questions and ideas inspired by Thomasine's story:

Contemplate the elements that define Beattie's sense of identity. Which do you have in your life? Which ones do you lack or want more of?

_____

_____

_____

_____

Where in your life are you setting aside your needs in order to avoid feeling guilty or disappointing others?

_____

_____

_____

What is it that you need in your life to make it more satisfying?

_____

_____

_____

Accept that you are not perfect, but know that you can handle whatever happens.

Identify the top five values that must be present in your life, such as honesty, integrity, family, etc. How do you honor these on a daily basis? Which ones do you want to see more of in your life?

_____

_____

_____

_____

Make your values the focal point of your life. Don't compromise them. At first, others may not like the new you, but you will sleep better at night knowing you stood up for what you believed in, and you'll start to see opportunities you never recognized before.

By knowing who you are and what you stand for, it becomes easier to find solutions to difficult decisions or situations.

Now that you've identified your top five values, what changes must you make in your life this week in order to cultivate the strength and presence of those values?

_____

_____

_____

_____

_____

Endnotes:

"Beyond Codependency: And Getting Better All the Time,"
by Melody Beattie (Hazelden).

Consultation with Joni Bury, MEd, CPCC; The Dream Network.

Sherry Shoemaker

Chapter Two:
Marirose Haffey

Being a victim doesn't leave a person with many options. You can stick it out in your pathetic situation, lick your wounds and blame the rest of the world for your problems, but taking this path of least resistance will cost you your self-respect and your integrity. And without those, who are you? For Marirose Haffey, standing by was simply not an option. Throughout her life, she's chosen to make decisions about her career, her marriages and her family that were far from easy. Sometimes those decisions worked out; sometimes they didn't. And while she still doesn't have her storybook ending, she wouldn't take back any of the hard choices she's made. They've been her road to empowerment. They've made her a survivor.

Growing up in an Irish Catholic household as an only child, Marirose and her mother held a deep and mutual adoration for one another. Her mother had a lot of great expectations for Marirose, and Marirose credits her wit, charisma and everything good about herself to her mother's influence. Marirose's father, on the other hand, remained an enigma. He seemed like a happy-go-lucky guy and the favorite uncle of all her cousins, but he remained emotionally distant from his daughter. Marirose can't even recall him ever extending so much as an, "I love you," to her.

The dynamic was not ideal under the best of circumstances, but when Marirose's mother died of heart disease when Marirose was just 17, things began to fall apart in earnest. Marirose was heartbroken and left with her dad, who coped with the loss by drinking heavily. This only made Marirose fearful of losing him, too, and so she stayed with him while she commuted to college in the Philadelphia area, making sure he got up in the morning for work and got into bed at the end of the day. But when she was 21, her father remarried, and her obligation to be his caretaker officially ended.

Yet the pattern was set: Marirose had begun to thrive on taking care of others. It gave her a feeling of importance and being needed, which may partly explain why she fell in love with Paul during her undergraduate career. He seemed like the perfect man for her — and he didn't drink! After they married, a professor persuaded them to move to New York City and major in film at Columbia University. She eventually landed a position as a casting assistant and editor for some prominent productions during the early '80s, and life seemed good. She thought she had found the perfect spouse and the perfect job. But after just three years of marriage, Marirose discovered Paul was a cocaine and sex addict.

Marirose was naive and believed Paul would change. During that time and place, after all, cocaine was all but ubiquitous, and Paul was good at hiding unpleasant habits. As a result, the marriage lasted eight years and produced a son named Daniel. But while she was on maternity leave, Marirose reached her breaking point with Paul. Fed up with his lies and manipulation, and devastated by his infidelity, she courageously ended the marriage then and there. It would've been easier to stick it out together, at least until Daniel was older, but she chose her integrity instead.

Unfortunately, that left her in the difficult position of

being a single mother. It was nearly impossible to survive on one salary in New York City, and the crazy hours of the film industry were hardly conducive to having a newborn at home. Divinely, a tenant from the apartment building Marirose and Paul supervised approached her about working as a communications officer at a nonprofit organization. She applied and got the job, and an elated and encouraged Marirose got her friends to watch Daniel while she worked. She missed her previous career in film, but she made the choice because she needed stability for herself and for Daniel more than achieving a professional dream.

By 1985, however, Marirose was facing yet another hard reality: She needed a better place to raise her son. Raising Daniel in New York City was not what she wanted for him. Reluctantly, she left behind her support system, moved back to Delaware County, Pennsylvania and took a position with another nonprofit where she soon met her second husband, Bill.

Bill was not a drinker, a drug user or a sex addict, and an ecstatic Marirose was sure that she'd gotten it right this time. Unfortunately, she eventually realized that Bill was a "dry drunk": He no longer drank alcohol but he did manifest all of the "isms" of an alcoholic. Self-centered, controlling and manipulative, Bill revealed, after three years of marriage, that he'd married Marirose so he would have the "intact" family he legally needed to take away the custodial rights of his ex-wife, who was also remarried. Bill also needed Marirose to take care of him, his home and his daughters. The patterns became eerily reminiscent of Paul, her father and the examples she'd seen all her life.

But things got worse before they got better. Bill stopped taking his medication for bipolar disorder and became abusive. With manic highs and depressive lows, he destroyed everything he touched: their home, his relationship with his daughters and his job, which he eventually lost. Shattered by his emotional abuse toward herself and her son, and suffering from the financial instability caused by Bill's reckless spending, Marirose wanted to leave. But the guilt of ending another marriage, combined with her father's religious-inspired insistence that she stay, held her back. Finally, she sought the advice of a Franciscan friar who was also a therapist. He advised her to save herself and her son from more misery and leave. After five years of marriage to Bill, Marirose left without a penny in her pocket. She and Daniel moved into an orphanage that employed Marirose as a fund raiser until she got back on her feet.

This was hard on Marirose, but in some ways it was even harder on Daniel, who longed to have a stable, supportive and loving father figure in his life. Instead, he had Paul who made guest appearances and, for a time, Bill, who was abusive. As an adolescent, this longing for a father figure led Daniel to befriend his soccer coach who went on to introduce him to alcohol. Even worse, this coach taught Daniel how to hide it. Daniel thrived under his coach's acceptance and attention, even as his "friend" set him on a ruinous path.

After about a year of successfully hiding an escalating habit, Daniel finally drank to the point of blacking out in the family room. That's where Marirose found him when she came home early from work. She frantically tried to wake him as she registered the stench of alcohol oozing from his body. Distraught, she realized she had another alcoholic on her hands. How could she miss the signs? What could she have done differently?

This was the beginning of 12 horrible years that would include several jail sentences as her son struggled with drug and alcohol addiction, and she struggled as the single parent of an addict.

The bright spot in all of this was Jack, a counselor who worked with Daniel early on and who shared the same Irish Catholic background as Marirose. He, too, was in recovery, and with similar values and background as Marirose, he grew particularly fond of Daniel, who reminded him of himself. Marirose could always count on Jack for advice and support with regard to Daniel, something that became especially valuable as her immediate and extended family began to shun them for their suffering.

After nine months of working with the counselor, Marirose desperately called Jack late one night about Daniel's addictive behavior. (Daniel had come home drunk and pushed Marirose down the steps.) Frantic as how to handle Daniel's alcohol-induced aggression, she called Jack. The advice he gave her, however, was not what she expected. He taught her how to fish. He told her about a program called Al-Anon and said she couldn't talk with him again until she'd attended five Al-Anon meetings. He didn't care if she went to five in one day, one a day for five days, one a week or one a month. But she did have to go to the meeting and, at the end, introduce herself to the chair who would write a note validating that she had attended.

She was livid! But it turned out to be the best gift she ever received. During the years her son was in jail, the Al-Anon program was her salvation. One friend from the program even made the eight-hour drive with her to West Virginia on the weekends to see Daniel in prison. Even now, 17 years later, she is still an Al-Anonic.

Though she couldn't see it at the time, Marirose had become as sick as the addicts in her life. She controlled, fixed others' lives and did whatever was possible to make a situation better for the addicts around her. Being raised in an alcoholic family had affected the way she coped with the world, but Al-Anon helped her rethink those destructive coping strategies.

To look at Marirose's life through one lens is to see sorrow and suffering. She grew up in an alcoholic household, her marriages ended and she suffered from abuse, financial loss and abandonment, even as she raised an addicted son as a single parent. She has yet to experience the joy and fulfillment of a romantic relationship founded on love rather than need.

And yet Marirose is not a pitiable character. She is not a victim. And that is one distinction that has very much been a conscious decision. Her experiences have given her the strength to know she can count on herself. If, she says, a person is open to what is presented and courageous enough to trust, that person will always have the choice to move forward.

Marirose's motto is still, "Let go and let God," even as she knows she must take an active role in living her life, making choices and maintaining her integrity. Integrity, she says, is the key to identity, and hers is very much one of survivorship. Today, she holds a position as the director of a local nonprofit that supports families on a daily basis. It is not a film career, but it is worthwhile and satisfying work. Her greatest blessing, however, is Daniel, who is in recovery, married, holding down a job and expecting his first child.

Reflections

Opportunity and possibilities, Marirose Haffey says, are everywhere — so long as you're not a victim. You have a choice to continue being a victim (and stay in the hell you're living), or break free. Breaking free, as Marirose did, means changing the rules about what you tell yourself. For example, do any of these rules sound familiar?

Don't:

Have fun

Put yourself first

Get close to people (it isn't safe)

Trust yourself or God

Set boundaries (because you may hurt other people's feelings)

Grow or change

Here are some examples of new rules that you can create for yourself. It is okay to:

Be direct

Be honest

Set boundaries

Speak your feelings

Put yourself first

Grow at your own pace

Let go and trust

Be imperfect

Changing what you want for yourself and how you act is akin to changing the dance with the others in your life. At first they may balk at the new you. You have, after all, changed the way you respond to their actions or requests. But we are allowed to take back our power! It may be scary and uncomfortable at first, but it will leave you empowered.

What new rules do you want to establish to release yourself from victim-hood? Write them out.

_____

_____

_____

_____

Recognize when you revert to the old rules, and
ask yourself:

What is the reason you revert to the old rules? Is it fear
or security?

_____

_____

_____

_____

How can you replace your old rule with your new rule?
What will you do differently? What will that feel like for
you? What type of person are you becoming?

_____

_____

_____

Surround yourself with people who will support you
through your transition, and ask your higher power for
help. There is something bigger than all of us that is in
control of our lives, states Marirose, and when you recognize that, grab onto it and start choosing integrity over
victim-hood. The possibilities will become endless.

Endnote:
"Beyond Codependency: And Getting Better All the Time,"
by Melody Beattie (Hazelden).

Sherry Shoemaker

Chapter Three:
Darla Pompilio

It was still dark outside when the alarm suddenly buzzed its morning greeting. Jumping out of bed, Darla paused a minute to remember where she was and that it was time to get ready for school. She didn't miss the morning hugs and kisses from her mom, because she'd never had them in the first place. Instead, as Darla made her own breakfast and packed her own lunch, she fretted over her mother who was passed out in bed. Whether from drinking or drugging, Darla didn't know, and it didn't much matter. The cause of her mother's unconsciousness may have varied from day to day, but the result was always the same: Before leaving for fifth grade, Darla would try to nudge her mom awake to make sure she was alive.

This was Darla Pompilio's life in the 1970s.

It would be easy to use these early years of abandonment as an excuse to justify Darla's own failures in the world. But Darla today looks at things differently. Instead of excusing herself — indeed, she hasn't failed but succeeded — Darla views her childhood as having been formative in an ultimately beneficial way. It wasn't perfect by any stretch of the imagination, but Darla used the good along with the bad to guide her own life in a positive direction.

Darla's mother struggled with drug and alcohol addiction for as long as Darla can remember. Sometimes the addiction would translate to passing out and leaving Darla to fend for herself; other times it would be more serious, like the two times she landed in jail. It was also the cause of a rootless existence: During her school years, Darla moved 16 times between California, Colorado and Indiana. The upside of this was that Darla became extremely self-sufficient. The downside, of course, was that her self-esteem and academic career were left in shambles. School for Darla was just someplace to go. She couldn't make friends — they moved around too much, and she felt too disconnected — and she never developed the right habits to study effectively. So after sleeping through classes, Darla would usually return to an empty house to clean, do laundry and make her own dinner.

Darla's wasn't a happy childhood, but neither was it dismal. There were times when Darla's mom was sober and able to connect with her daughter, and these are Darla's happiest memories. Her mom, she remembers, was loving and fun to be around. In fact, while her mom's substance abuse created significant problems for Darla, she still always felt grateful that her mom wasn't mean, even if she wasn't entirely reliable either. She knew her mother loved her, and this counted for more than stability with Darla.

During Darla's childhood, her mom managed to earn a computer-science degree, but taking care of herself was often all she was capable of doing. So when her mom was away for long periods of time, or when Darla just needed some company, Darla and her younger half-sister, Gina, would turn either to their maternal grandmother or to Darla's personal favorite, their Aunt Jackie.

Jackie wasn't technically related — she was a close friend of Darla's mom — but where Darla's grandmother was grouchy and judgmental (if stable), Jackie was supportive, fun and a good moral compass. Darla didn't want to grow up to be like her mom, and Jackie taught her the manners and social skills she could never learn on her own. (Her grandmother, for all her old-fashioned ideas, wasn't much help in this arena either.)

By the time Darla was 18, her mom had moved back in the house after a prolonged absence but was still drinking and using drugs. Darla, who just wanted to escape the chaos, knew she could do better living on her own, especially since she could hold a steady job. So she moved in with her boyfriend, her only regret being that she had to leave behind her half-sister.

Darla lived with her boyfriend for the next three years, earning decent money in the restaurant business. But eventually she felt like her circumstances were controlling her life rather than the other way around, and so she packed up her things once again to move. She left her hometown and her boyfriend in southern Indiana and eventually relocated to Indianapolis. There, she was able to afford a comfortable apartment and night school, an enterprise that didn't come easy but at which Darla nonetheless persevered in order to make her life better.

Along with her study habits, Darla's self-confidence was also improving. She joined fitness classes, and started building friendships and trusting other people for support. She was determined not to fail, but she didn't know how to succeed. So her method for success became living her life the opposite way her mother did. She shed the victim role, chose to be happy and acted accordingly. "Attitude is everything,"

Darla explains, "and happiness is a choice."

By the time she was 32, Darla realized that some of her romantic choices were leading her down the wrong path. She saw a disturbing pattern of selfishness and alcohol abuse in her previous boyfriends that only left her disappointed. Case in point was the man Darla dated for three years and planned on marrying until she discovered he was cheating on her. Darla's response? To kick him out immediately. She didn't look back. She didn't want to be like her mom.

After that, Darla decided to see a therapist. She was ready to move to the next level in her life and get a secure job, a degree and, hopefully, a husband. Therapy taught her that she needed to trust herself, and this resonated with what her Aunt Jackie had always told her: that one day God would send her the man she wanted.

Still in Indianapolis and working, Darla and her Aunt Jackie drove out to New Jersey to see Gina who was attending Rutgers University at the time. During that trip, Midwestern Darla fell in love with New York City. The restaurants, ethnic diversity, Broadway shows, proximity to the beach and skiing — New York had it all as far as Darla was concerned, and she felt reborn. As soon as she saved enough money, she decamped to this newfound home on her own. Fear didn't strike until she arrived and came face to face with some mighty culture shock. The pace was faster, the people were more highly strung and the cost of living was in a different stratosphere. The last of these meant she had to find another job besides working at a restaurant, so she went to Revlon and applied for a position as a lab tech. "I'm smart and can do what you want me to do, so hire me," Darla told the interviewer. Darla got the job.

Darla worked there for three years, before moving to Colgate. After she graduated school with a degree in exercise science, she landed a job at Merck doing wellness screening for companies nationwide. The company was understaffed, and she was overloaded. So while she was finally making money, it came at the expense of her personal well-being. Going to bed at midnight and getting up at 4 a.m. was draining her, and she began to dream of the day she could have her own company. Finally, in 2008, Darla took a pay cut for a better lifestyle: She quit her job to start a concierge business, which essentially handles errands and tasks for people who don't have the time to do them themselves.

Darla knew that if she could survive the first year, things would be okay. By this time she'd married Lou, the man her Aunt Jackie had promised would come. Lou fully supported Darla emotionally when she moved forward with her dream, as did the rest of her family. But because he worked as a musician and didn't make much money, Darla knew she couldn't afford to strike out on her own on a whim. Still, her previous life and work experience had vested her with the right business background, not to mention the skill set necessary to organize and help other people manage their lives. Most importantly, however, Darla finally knew how to trust. She trusted herself and her intuition, and so she started her business, Your Tasks — Our Time, LLC, in 2008. Darla not only survived her first year in business, she did better than she'd hoped. More determined than ever to make it work, Darla hired a business coach and doubled her business in two years!

Darla's life challenges have helped her in many ways. She is firmly grounded, no matter what comes her way; and when she sets her mind to something, she refuses to take no for an answer. Perhaps more than anything else, though, she trusts. She trusts her husband, her God and herself to make the decisions that will lead her life in the direction she wants. So far, that trust has rewarded her with the life, marriage and career she's always wanted.

Reflections

Darla knew early on that she didn't want to be a victim, but it took her a lifetime to fine-tune her approach to empowering herself. As she grew personally, she conquered her fears of becoming just like her mom or of not being good enough to attain the goals she wanted. While each person's circumstances may be vastly different from Darla's, everyone knows what it's like to fear. And many times our fears trick us into accepting the status quo, whether it's a destructive relationship or an unfulfilled career, by whispering untruths to us like, "This is just the way it is." Or, "I am not good/pretty/smart enough for what I want." Once, like Darla, you see those fears for what they are, you can take the chances that lead you away from fear and into a fulfilling life.

So how do you start overcoming your fears? With these straightforward questions:

Where in your life is fear holding you back?

_____

_____

_____

If you had no fears, where would you be or what would you have? A new career? A new mate? Would you be back at school?

_____

_____

What are your fears costing you? Serenity? A fulfilling relationship or career?

_____

_____

_____

What is it that you regret not doing because you fear the outcome or hurting others?

_____

_____

_____

Only you are in control of your life, which means only you are responsible for its current state. You can't blame anybody else. So where in your life are you not taking responsibility? In relationships? In your career?

_____

_____

_____

Where in your life can you rise above the fear and take responsibility?

_____

_____

_____

What corrections must be made to live a happy life?

_____

_____

_____

_____

Sometimes negative chatter comes into our heads and wreaks havoc. For instance, maybe you're tempted to move to Paris because you've always wished you could. Maybe you're finally on the cusp of doing it when your doubts set in, telling you things like, "Don't move out of town! It's hard to make money there. You're too old to do that anyway." Or maybe you tell yourself not to be so pushy, or that no one appreciates you or that you're not good enough for whatever it is you want. You get the idea.

But where does this get you in the long run? Nowhere! Instead of remaining a victim, you must take responsibility for what you want out of your life. The time to do something is now. Make sure you do your homework, gather all the facts about your undertaking, set realistic and achievable goals and TRUST that you can handle whatever may come your way.

If you could wave a magic wand and remove all obstacles, what would you want for yourself in each of these areas?

Family and friends

Career

Physical environment

Health

Personal growth

Romance

Money

Fun and recreation

Now that you have your wish list, you can write your goals. What is one step that will get you closer to your vision? For example, let's say you want to change jobs but have to go back to school in order to do so. Make that call today to find out more about the curriculum. Do this for each of the eight areas listed above, and schedule a daily time on your calendar to work on each of them.

It's time to step through your fears. Whatever the outcome, you will inevitably learn something about yourself or your accomplishment, and you'll be one step closer to living the life you want.

"Don't be afraid to take a big step when one is indicated. You can't cross a chasm in two small jumps." — David Lloyd George

---

Endnotes:

Portions of this section were informed by the following texts:

"Feel the Fear...and Do It Anyway," by Susan Jeffers, Ph.D. (Ballantine Books, 2007).

"Stand Up for Your Life: A Practical Step-by-Step Plan to Build Inner Confidence and Personal Power," by Cheryl Richardson (Free Press, 2002).

Chapter Four:
Barbara Marte

For most of us, "Erin Brockovich" was a memorable movie about a courageous, modern-day fighter who took on a David-and-Goliath type challenge...and won. We don't know anyone like that in real life, of course, but it sure makes a good story.

The thing is, Erin Brockovich is a real person and — here's the best part — there are more real people just like her. People who are strong and unwilling to compromise when they are trying to right a wrong. People who are like Barbara Marte, a general-duty RN who took on doctors, lawyers and insurance companies to stop the abuse she saw in the health care system.

Like most heroines of this day and age, Barbara didn't set out to overhaul the system, but she did receive some pivotal lessons early on. Like the one in which her parents modeled the belief that you don't allow life to happen, you make life happen. For Barbara, that meant listening to her inner voice urging her to be the best person she could be and to work in a capacity that would benefit others. That voice led her to move from rural York County, Pennsylvania to Philadelphia so she could attend Lankenau Hospital School of Nursing.

Upon completing her three-year nursing degree, Barbara married, had three children and worked part-time in a hospital as a registered RN until her youngest child entered first grade. Wanting to take on a full-time position, Barbara anxiously applied to be the director of nursing at a small, long-term care facility. To her surprise, she got the job!

At first, Barbara loved it. She benefited from some great mentors who helped her get the lay of the land. But as she settled into her new role, she began to realize there were tremendous inequities in the system, and patients were not getting the care they needed. If a patient had Post traumatic Stress Disorder (PTSD), for example, he might seem to the outside world like he was fine when in reality he suffered on a daily basis. These patients, however, would be routinely denied help — something that infuriated Barbara. Services, Barbara discovered, were cut and dry: They were meant to attend to a patient's immediate and visible needs, but there was little regard for his/her emotional ones.

Barbara knew she wanted to make operating changes, and she drew on the lessons from her childhood to make them. She realized that if, as a clinician, you want to talk to board members or facility owners, you need to learn their language. At that time, it was the '80s, and in Barbara's facility, the language was budget. Undeterred, Barbara built her case by fact-finding, researching both sides of recovery time, examining her facility's statistics, evaluating staff satisfaction and talking to outside professionals. Furthermore, she did this while working 24/7 to keep her facility running smoothly. Finally, with considerable perseverance, Barbara was able to present her petition to overhaul service protocol and return legitimacy to patient care. The board was impressed, but the challenge then was as it would continue to be: Providing quality patient care with limited financial resources.

Barbara loved her job, but she eventually grew frustrated with the hours she was spending away from her children, all to provide what she considered fiscally-constrained substandard care. If she were going to sacrifice her family time, it had to be for a better cause. She wanted to make treatment plans legitimately effective. She wanted her patients to get better and go back to work. And when she could no longer tolerate not meeting those standards, she left her position.

She wasn't, however, unemployed for long: Her next job was in case management for patients, a position where she thought she might make a difference in patient care and still spend more time with her family. Again she had to undergo a new education, this time about the insurance industry, and develop a plan that would help patients and her employer alike. For example, she met one truck driver who'd injured his knee and needed an evaluation for workman's compensation. While he sat in the waiting room, another patient observed, "Oh, that injury is good for six months to a year of compensation." Barbara's job was to stop such predatory behavior where people simply relied on longer-term compensation and only dealt with rehabilitation and returning to work once the checks stopped coming. It was her job to motivate those patients to get back to work or tell her insurance company that a person simply wasn't going to get better.

Barbara was up against more than apathetic patients, though. At that time, attorneys and doctors profited when patients stayed on long-term care. This was yet another abuse that aggravated Barbara. Not only was it dishonest, it was lazy and wasteful, creating financial benefits for few and loss of life and purpose for many.

Barbara knew there had to be a way to get patients back to work, especially when they were suffering from a head injury or PTSD. As she saw in her first director position, those patients often had their claims denied because they weren't demonstrably ill. So Barbara got creative, like when she came across a patient whose memory issues prevented her from attending school. As a case manager, Barbara acquired a computer for her and classified it as a prosthesis so that insurance would pay for it. (The "prosthesis" acted as an aide for the patient's brain.) Examples like this fueled Barbara's desire for reform, she eventually became a specialist in head injury while studying with researchers. This background helped her develop a research-based plan of care for patients suffering from head injuries, which was purchased by a long-term care company that hired Barbara as well.

Now working for a long-term care facility, Barbara was reminded daily that cost-effective measures were top priority. Each patient was allocated a fixed amount of money per day for care. This amount increased if the patient were on Medicare, and decreased if s/he were paying out of pocket or had private insurance. When things were well-funded, this plan made sense. Thanks to Barbara's plan, care now included cognitive stimulation and meeting emotional needs alongside preventive health and wellness care, as well as making sure each patient was attended to according to his/her needs. But when a facility had to make budget cuts, everything went awry because it always started with cutting staff.

So Barbara and the C.F.O. of this long-term care facility approached it from a different angle. Instead of hiring as much staff as a budget would allow, Barbara created a system of resource allocation. This meant, in other words, putting patients who needed more care on a floor that would be heavily staffed, while patients needing less care would be placed together on a different floor with less staff.

Barbara could've stopped there. She'd taken on the system and proved her way was better. But precisely because she knew her way was better, and because she had such a passion for delivering better patient care, she went on the lecture circuit to other long-term-care facilities. Not only was this a way to spread positive change, it also allowed her to spend more time with her family.

Of course, plenty of facilities balked at her proposal. She knew this would happen if only from her previous job experiences. But she also knew that science is hard to refute, and so she scientifically presented the results of how her care plan improved patient health. She didn't give up.

Barbara felt so strongly that patients could be helped within any given facility's budget that she went on to tailor her plan for nursing homes specializing in sub-acute care, so that more people might benefit from her expertise. But, as with every other position she would take from then on out, once she realized that her company was more concerned with the almighty dollar than patient care, she quit in disgust. She refused to compromise her belief that patient care trumps any other concern, and that it can be provided in an economical way.

Today, more than 40 years after she began her career as a nurse, Barbara owns her own company: Seniors Helping Seniors. The company, which Barbara laughingly refers to as her retirement, provides in-home service from seniors to other seniors. Finally, Barbara has found a professional contentment that eluded her when battling big companies over budgets. "As people get older, they become invisible," she says. "We make them [feel] important and feel productive [but let them] stay in their homes."

Barbara is in charge of herself now, and likes that she doesn't have to listen to the powers that be. While she earned a bigger paycheck working in the corporate world, she enjoys other benefits now, like the sense that she can personally touch lives, the ability to develop her own corporate discipline and the chance to make a positive difference in senior care. This, she says, is a step in the right direction that is mutually beneficial. "We respect them," Barbara says of her those in her care, "are patient and love them for who they are."

Looking back, Barbara is able to see how the trajectory of her life has followed certain touchstones. For starters, she emphasizes, you have to just go for it when you see a need that you can meet. Don't wait for somebody else to do the job, and don't waste time feeling intimidated. After all, you can always empower yourself by learning what you need to succeed through fact-finding, going back to school and talking to others who are doing what you want to do. This examination of both sides of an issue is important for broadening your perspective and informing your actions.

Once you know who you are and what you stand for, Barbara says, don't compromise. You have to let go and have faith that everything will work out because, in the end, isn't life happening perfectly as planned?

Reflections

Barbara felt so much enthusiasm for her patients that she developed the courage to change the system of patient care so her patients could recover well and quickly. Whenever a facility would block her efforts by putting budgets ahead of patients, Barbara relied on her integrity to fight back or leave. If she had to leave, she moved on to a different facility and even took her program on the road, changes that required endurance. Eventually, all this paid off when a long-term care facility bought her plan, and other facilities, after seeing how patients got better and staff felt more satisfied, followed suit.

Having enthusiasm, courage, integrity and endurance led Barbara to live according to the principles and standards thoughtfully outlined by Ron Renaud in his book, "The Uncompromised." As described in "The Uncompromised," we must have enthusiasm and positive energy or else we relinquish our power to life's circumstances.

Where in your life can you bring more enthusiasm to create positive energy?

_____

_____

_____

_____

What steps can you take now to create that change? Is it recognizing those negative thoughts as old tapes and creating new, positive ones? Or expressing gratitude for what is good in your life? Or finding a support group with positive, energetic people? Or maybe you need to get rid of toxic people in your life? Chances are, there's someplace in your life that needs a fresh, enthusiastic approach.

In order to create change, you need courage to step through any fear and stand up for what you feel is right, just as Barbara did. People may not like the new you. They may challenge you or even fire you from your job. So you have to ask yourself the following:

What is so urgent that you will override your fear?

_____

_____

_____

_____

What do you want from your life?

_____

_____

_____

What will it cost you to get it?

_____

_____

_____

Once you understand the cost and nature of courage, you must develop endurance, or the ability to withstand hardship. Nobody said it would be easy to stand up for your beliefs and pursue them. Endurance involves perseverance and planning. It is a conscious choice that we make daily in order to live the uncompromised life that we deserve.

What do you want to achieve in life? Set aside a time to create a plan with a starting and finishing time.

_____

_____

_____

How will you achieve it? Start by creating a vision for yourself with attainable goals. If they aren't attainable and realistic, they just won't work for you.

_____

_____

_____

What obstacles will you have to surmount along the way? There will be obstacles, and if you plan for them and persevere, you will succeed. Otherwise life's circumstances will run your life for you.

_____

_____

_____

In order to be truthful to yourself and your plan, you must proceed with integrity. Without being true to your goals, you will fold under pressure and criticism from others. As Ralph Waldo Emerson said, "It is easy to live for others, everybody does. I call on you to live for yourself."

What role does integrity play in your life?

_____

_____

_____

What plan must you create to live a life that honors yourself? Is it eating healthy? Standing up for what you believe at work? Or at home? Not keeping secrets? Saying no even when you really don't want to disappoint others?

_____

_____

_____

Your actions speak louder than your words. You are worthy of living true to your purpose. Now go for it!

Endnote:
"The Uncompromised," by Ron Renaud (Washington Franklin Publishing Paperback, 2011)

Sherry Shoemaker

Chapter Five:
Sharon Snyder

Time passed slowly one February night in 1998 as Sharon and Bob Snyder waited with their 23-month-old son, Kyle, in a private hospital room in Meadowbrook, Pennsylvania. It was cold outside and well into the evening, and the Snyders were anxious to receive Kyle's latest test results. Sharon held her son close, praying that they'd finally figure out the problem — and that it would be easily cured. Suddenly, Kyle's pediatrician walked through the door. What is she doing here on a Friday night? Sharon wondered. How nice of her to check in on Kyle! Then it hit her: Kyle's doctor wasn't just being kind. She was responding to a serious situation.

As the pediatrician approached them, Sharon shouted, "No! I can't hear this. You need to leave the room. If you give me the test results of why Kyle is sick, it makes it real." She felt like the floor was opening up and sucking her into a big, dark hole. The pediatrician spoke quietly. "I am really sorry," she said, "but Kyle has leukemia, and you must go to The Children's Hospital of Philadelphia to properly diagnosis his illness right away." Sharon fell to the floor in disbelief. She started screaming and crying, wondering if Kyle was going to die that night, while Bob held their son and stood in disbelief. Their world had turned upside down.

As Sharon sees it, there were two stages in Kyle's abbreviated life: Before he got sick and after. Before his diagnosis, Kyle went to daycare, had play dates with friends and led the sort of carefree existence that defines childhood. Then one day Bob was bathing Kyle and noticed bruises on his son's legs. Soon after, Bob and Sharon found spots on Kyle's chest. They began taking him to doctors to find out what was wrong, but no one had an answer. Sharon was beside herself. She knew this wasn't just a rash, so she called and insisted on an appointment with their Pediatrician. She needed answers.

Sharon, an attractive and petite brunette with a kind and gracious smile, is the kind of dynamo who seems never to stop going. Her boundless energy and enthusiasm are in step with motherhood and all its demands. In fact, Sharon had wanted to be a mom for as long as she could remember. Her own upbringing had been less than perfect with a mother who suffered from mental and physical illnesses and an emotionally absent father. Sharon, however, was determined to do things differently. When she gave birth to Kyle on March 15, 1996, she felt a connection with him that transcended, she says, ordinary parent-child relationships. Often people consider their spouses to be their soul mates. For Sharon, however, a soul mate wasn't romantic but something more intense and lasting, a role only Kyle could fill. She loved her husband, but Kyle provided something for her that no one had been able to before. She would simply stare at Kyle for hours and was, as she puts it, in awe of his beauty and the power of his soul and spirit.

When it was time for Sharon to go back to work, it was difficult to leave her son. Her whole life revolved around this wonderful creation, and she wanted to be with him all the time. Some of her family and friends criticized her for not going anywhere without him, but Sharon was just as baffled by cultural norms. But circumstances demanded Sharon return to her job as a massage therapist and so, at 18 months old, Kyle entered daycare.

Then Kyle got sick, and his life went from days filled with playing and learning to enduring spinal taps, chemotherapy, oral medications and countless pokes and prods. The day Kyle was diagnosed, Sharon quit her job to care for him. Money, she discovered, was no longer her top concern; being with her son at this critical time in his life was. "I don't believe that everything happens for a reason," Sharon explains. "I don't believe in the theory that God does not give you more than you can handle. I don't believe God caused Kyle's sickness. I look at myself as a person with free will who gets to make my own decisions." And all anyone can do, Sharon realized, is respond to each situation as it arises in the best way possible.

This attitude meant that, upon receiving Kyle's diagnosis, Sharon began to soak up information about leukemia. Beforehand, childhood cancer was the sort of thing that happened in movies, not real life. At least not in her life. She found, however, that there are several forms of childhood leukemia, and the doctors diagnosed Kyle with Acute Lymphoblastic Leukemia (ALL), As Sharon describes it, bone marrow produces a person's blood, specifically the platelets and the red and white blood cells. Once produced, the cells enter the bloodstream, and when they die off, the bone marrow produces new cells. For people with leukemia, the marrow might produce one cell that, inexplicably, never matures but enters the bloodstream anyway. Every cell after that replicates it. By the time Kyle was diagnosed after just a couple weeks of showing symptoms, the doctors estimated that 98 percent of his bone marrow was filled with immature cells. At that time, the diagnosis carried a 67-percent cure rate. It wasn't what the Snyders wanted to hear, but at least they could hope.

Over the next eight months, Bob and Sharon lived on that hope of recovery. Every day, Sharon told her son that all of the stuff he was going through was to make him feel better. Privately, though, she couldn't shake the thought, What if it doesn't? This was the best that they had, and the situation was miserable. Kyle, however, responded well to the chemotherapy, and instead of being in the hospital for a month, he was home in 10 days.

Three weeks after his diagnosis, Kyle celebrated his second birthday. Sharon decided to have a small celebration with just immediate family as she tried to keep things as normal as possible. She was elated Kyle was home, even though he was still on chemo meds and swollen from the steroids. While she also longed for the normalcy of a big birthday party with kids, games and all the excitement, she realized this was her new norm for the time being. And the most important thing was that her little boy was still alive.

Although Kyle initially responded well to the chemo-therapy, it didn't last. "We suddenly realized that something wasn't working," Sharon recalls. It turned out the leukemia was in the central nervous system. It was a devastating discovery. At initial diagnosis, they didn't treat the central nervous system. Sharon wonders if Kyle's chances for survival would've been considerably higher had this occured. Instead, they had to bombard his body with even more intensive treatments in an effort to cure his cancer. His chances for survival dropped dramatically.

Through tears, Sharon remembers, "He was the happiest kid. I still adore him so much. I never understood how my parents could put me aside at times and not appreciate me, and I knew that when I had kids, they would be treasured. Then this happens."

Just eight months after his second birthday, and despite the intensified treatments, Kyle suffered a relapse, and his condition became grave. In the middle of the night on October 15, 1998, Kyle went into shock and then several hours later, suddenly, died. "We didn't expect it," Sharon says. One moment, she felt and heard her son and sensed his reassuring presence in the room with her. The next moment, he was gone.

Days before Kyle passed away, Sharon had a dream in which Kyle was sitting in a chair in a field of vivid greens, oranges and yellows while nurses were saying to Sharon, "He's okay." Sharon felt peaceful, even though she was being prepared for the worst. When she woke up, the panic returned, a fear that was justified by his death only a few days later.

Later that year, Sharon's mom was diagnosed with terminal cancer and a year later passed away from cancer, too. Sharon had lost her past and her present within two years. She was submerged in agony. How could she go on? She experienced glimpses of peace, like when she was in Kyle's room and noticed three ladybugs (his favorite) on his window screen, a sign she interpreted as his spirit staying close to her. But for the most part, depression set in, and Sharon, who had once been a put-together woman, could hardly get out of bed each morning.

But Sharon knew that somehow she had to keep Kyle's spirit alive, and being depressed in bed all day just wasn't going to do it. She went to therapy and worked through the gut-wrenching pain of losing a child. She felt she needed to feel every moment, not escape through drugs, alcohol or any other substance she felt would prevent her from working through her grief. She knew, deep inside, that this experience would be important for helping others going through the same thing. She relied on the sense that Kyle's spirit was guiding her to give her the strength and courage to move forward and help others in her son's name.

Eventually Sharon found the best way for her to keep Kyle's spirit alive was to volunteer. She started a memorial fund in Kyle's name within a month of his passing. The funds raised were donated to causes associated to childhood cancer such as the Oncology floor at CHOP and The Ronald McDonald House. She also volunteered at the Leukemia & Lymphoma Society. As time passed, she realized this wasn't enough for her to work through her grief. She needed to find a way to be able to take care of Kyle on a daily basis in the present. To have him continue on and not a memory of something that once was. The result was **Kisses for Kyle**, a foundation she began in 2001, whose name plays off of Kyle's initials,

KSS. The Kisses for Kyle Foundation helps families whose children are battling cancer, birth through 21, from the moment of diagnosis all the way through post treatment.

Sharon found that raising money and helping others gave her a sense of purpose, an elation that almost resembled an emotional fix. "It was this great high" she says. During her time of volunteering, it made her heart and spirit feel alive again. More importantly, she senses that Kyle's spirit was guiding her every time she helped.

While Sharon's impact is far-reaching, she stays close to her roots. She runs Kisses for Kyle from her home. She personally knows many of the families she assists. Perhaps this direct approach is what attracts others to her work. Local sports teams, for example, like the Philadelphia Flyers and the Philadelphia Eagles have pitched in to help her cause in ways such as sending players to support fundraisers and events.

Because of such support, Sharon is realizing her vision of making the world a better place and keeping Kyle's spirit alive while she does it. Through Kisses for Kyle, many children and their families benefit directly from Sharon's compassion, empathy and financial aid. For more information about the organization, go to **www.kissesforkyle.org**.

Reflections

In reaching her lowest point and struggling to find her way back up, Sharon learned many lessons. The most powerful of these can be boiled down to a single philosophy: "We are all human," she says. "Take the pity and the ego out of it, and help each other. That is what we are all here for. To make a difference."

Sharon lives by this philosophy and you can, too. Consider the following:

Think of a time when you made a difference in somebody's life. What did that feel like for you? What positive attributes were you exhibiting?

_____

_____

_____

_____

Where in your life are you making a difference today? In the lives of others or in your community?

_____

_____

_____

_____

_____

What is most important about that for you?

_____

_____

_____

_____

What values are you honoring when you serve?
For Sharon, she honored her values of family, the
responsibility to help others and the commitment to
make the world a better place. Do you honor similar
values or different ones?

_____

_____

_____

_____

What have you learned about yourself when you actively
make a difference in the world?

_____

_____

_____

_____

If you aren't making a difference, what is holding you back? What do you need to create that change in your life?

_____

_____

_____

_____

_____

Chapter Six:
Tracy Dougherty

Whether we admit it or not, we all carry emotional baggage that affects us on a daily basis. Luckily for us, we also all carry the power to shed that baggage and live healthier, happier lives. Don't buy it? Then meet Tracy Dougherty, a woman who refused to accept victim-hood, even after surviving a childhood of abuse.

Tracy and her two siblings grew up with a mom who suffered from borderline personality disorder and a dad who spent most weeks away on business. (Borderline personality disorder commonly features aggression, impulsive behavior, emotional instability, suspiciousness and unexpected mood swings.) Since Tracy's older sister spent a lot of time outside the home with an aunt, and since Tracy's brother also suffered from borderline personality disorder, Tracy emerged as the caretaker of the family. Her mother was jealous whenever Tracy paid attention to someone other than herself. Her brother, Scott, meanwhile, resented the attention his otherwise indifferent mother showered on Tracy. As a result, he terrorized his sister in a number of ways, like pushing her into traffic and pulling her out just before a car struck her, or holding her out a window as though to drop her.

Yet for all the abuse Scott heaped on her, Tracy recognized the bright, sweet, creative kid underneath the illness. In moments of lucidity, he was even likeable. But Tracy also realized Scott was the victim of a different abuse. In addition to borderline personality disorder, he suffered from ADD and dyslexia, disorders that led his parents to reject and even ridicule him. By tolerating his abuse and acting as a surrogate parent, Tracy helped prevent him from getting into further trouble.

It was a strategy that worked until Scott grew up and became more aggressive. If Tracy asked for intervention from her dad when he was home on a weekend, he'd simply retort, "Don't make that little kid squeak." He was not Tracy's ally, which meant Tracy was on her own to protect her brother from her mom and to take care of him.

Yet Tracy's mom also needed help. Indeed, much of Tracy's day-to-day existence was spent pitching in with household chores, tending to her younger brother's needs and reassuring her mom that everything would be okay. (She did this so well, in fact, that her mother managed to earn two master's degrees while Tracy was growing up.) Nothing, however, was okay. If she wasn't worrying that her brother might kill her one day, and if she wasn't fretting about how her mother might react to any given situation, then Tracy was refereeing physical fights between her parents. Her father may have only been around on the weekends, but he managed to pack a lot of drama into those two days. Tracy remembers standing by like a little soldier, ready to step in, as she watched her 110-pound mother physically attack her 200-pound, ex-professional-boxer husband.

Surprisingly, nobody ever told her to leave. Not even when, on one Friday night, a teenage Tracy watched as wedding rings were flushed down the toilet and clothes were thrown across the room and out the window. Screaming in fit of rage, Tracy's dad held her mom in a choke hold. Tracy could see her mom's face turning red, and her father's fury showed no signs of abating. Incensed and horrified, Tracy sprang into action. She slammed her body into her father's with a strength that only fear could summon, and knocked him to the ground. Dazed, her father heaved himself up and both parents retreated in the dead silence. As her heart pounded with adrenaline, Tracy remained vigilant on the sofa that night to prevent any further confrontations.

Despite the emotional toll of their behaviors, Tracy loved her mother and brother dearly. In her heart, she felt more compassion for them than she did for herself. And while selflessness and compassion can be desirable traits to cultivate, Tracy took it too far. Her identity and self-esteem gradually melted into her relationship with her mom and Scott, a fact that ultimately led her to tolerate the abuse.

With a significant amount of trepidation, Tracy decided to go to away to college, and she eventually graduated with a degree in elementary education. Yet being in college forced Tracy to realize that, after taking care of two other people so completely, she was left with no identity of her own. If she recognized a trait from her mother or father in herself, she'd panic, wondering, Will I be like them? So when she graduated, she left home for a teaching position in Texas, figuring that putting some distance between her childhood and her adulthood might help her get a grip on who she was. The experience, however, lasted only a few years. She'd simply transferred her need to care for her family to needing to care for her students. But because she was used to fulfilling every need of two people, she felt compelled to meet every need of the children in her care, a drive that emotionally drained her.

By the time she was 25, she returned to Pennsylvania to care again for her needy mother and brother. She eventually married and had a son, but functioning in a so-called "normal" family situation was foreign to her. And she was exhausted from a lifetime spent anxiously avoiding confrontations. So by the time her son was 3, just doing daily household chores became a burden. Night sweats from PTSD and rage engulfed her as she tried desperately to function as a mom. Her past was threatening to overwhelm her, and yet Tracy knew that she didn't want her child to grow up in a tumultuous environment. So she decided to see a therapist who helped her cope with her anger. But as her rage subsided, a heavy depression sank in. Just taking care of her 3-year-old was a chore. No medication seemed to work; all she wanted to do was sleep.

For 10 years, Tracy lived under this cloud. While raising her son (and facing down the start of his matriculation into middle school), and while managing the needs of her husband and home, Tracy was also still coping with the antics of her mom. On the surface, her mother seemed to have it together: She'd divorced Tracy's dad and was working part-time as a geriatric social worker. At the age of 71, she drove up to Vermont by herself to join a cycling trip, suffered a major heart attack while biking and died before being revived. As she lay comatose in a Vermont hospital on life-support, Tracy and her sister flew up to see her. After four days, they decided to remove the feeding tube and respirator. Yet their mother miraculously survived and, after 24 hours, she woke up smiling.

But time proved all was not well. Her mother was delusional, brain damaged and psychotic. Nobody expected her to live. She spent 28 days in rehab before entering Tracy's care, a move that lasted just four weeks. When her mother, convinced the house was on fire, tried to jump out of a second-story window, Tracy reluctantly committed her to a psychiatric ward. She made daily visits to her mother until the nurses told her it wasn't necessary. At that point, Tracy was able to devote more attention to her brother, who was divorced, unemployed and at home drinking all day, constantly calling her for help. Once again, Tracy felt alone. Her husband, while empathetic, traveled frequently for business, leaving Tracy on her own to battle depression, care for her son and assume responsibility for the emotional well-being of her mother and brother.

This turned out to be her final hurdle. She bounced from therapist to psychiatrist to therapist, gaining 40 pounds in one year and gleaning no useful insight into who she was or what she wanted. It wasn't until her brother passed away from alcoholism at 51, and her mother passed away from a heart attack, that Tracy finally found a psychiatrist who clicked with her. Suddenly she had someone who would talk, listen and validate. More importantly, she'd found someone who hit upon the right combination of medicine that made Tracy feel alive again.

Once in her 50s, and with the right diagnosis and medication, Tracy was finally able to profit from therapy. (In fact, she's a firm believer in the importance of finding a good therapist who can help you understand your childhood and how it affects you today.) She was far enough away from her past to recognize that her unconditional love for her mother and brother arose out of her desperate need not to be abandoned. She had sacrificed her childhood and a good portion of her adulthood to this pattern and to the guilt of not being able to do more for them. It was time to heal with therapy, new patterns and introspection.

Today, Tracy is most proud of how she raised her son and how she continues to have close relationship with him. She has broken the cycle of her past, treasuring him the way she wishes she and her siblings had been cherished by their parents. She knew what she didn't want for her son, but what she gave him — the chance to develop his own identity within a quiet, loving household — was as much a lesson for her as it was an opportunity for him.

As Tracy puts it, now it's, "My turn, my time." If her childhood and early adulthood were fractious, contentious and painful, she was determined her professional life would be the opposite. She'd always appreciated beauty — a benefit of having regularly visited the art museum with her mom — and she'd always loved flowers. It was only natural, then, that she begin a silk-flower business, which she did in 2010. The quiet, lasting beauty of her creations today echoes the patterns of the new life she's made for herself and replaces the darkness and chaos of her past.

Reflections

How has your past affected your behavior over the years? Or, more to the point, what aspects of your past do you keep closeted in the recesses of your mind? Is it an abusive childhood? Addictions, mental illness or victim-hood? How does it feel to carry this weight? Do you worry about sharing it for fear that others won't understand or, worse, that you will have to admit it was real and deal with it? Or are you swimming in a sea of denial and making rash justifications for your behavior?

Whatever your particular situation, you probably feel hemmed in by that internal voice we all have that seems to protect us but really just keeps us from making meaningful changes in our lives. It might tell us we can't do something or that we're not good enough, usually when we're just about to step out of our comfort zone and try something that will ultimately help us.

In Tracy Dougherty's case, her past informed much of her adulthood as she drifted through life as a victim, a depressed mother and a guilt-ridden caretaker before she assumed ownership of her history and future and turned her life around. She stopped being the victim. We all have the power to, as Tracy did, end our victim-hood.

Here's where it starts.

Make a list of everything you tell yourself when you are stepping out of your comfort zone or doing something for yourself. From your list, ask yourself these four questions as outlined in Byron Katie's "Loving What Is: Four Questions That Can Change Your Life":

Is it true?

_____

_____

_____

Can you absolutely know that it's true?

_____

_____

_____

How do you react, what happens, when you believe that thought?

_____

_____

_____

Who would you be without the thought?

_____

_____

_____

Now, coming from what is available to you without all those negative thoughts, use Melody Beattie's thoughtful questions from "Codependent No More: How to Stop Controlling Others and Take Care of Yourself," and journal about the following:

How do you feel about changing yourself?

_____

_____

_____

_____

What would happen if you changed?

_____

_____

_____

Do you think you can change?

_____

_____

_____

Drawing on Tracy's attitude of, "My turn, my time," what is the first step that you can take to live a life for yourself without guilt?

_____

_____

_____

_____

Once you decide how you want to change, find a positive support group to cheer you on, and trust that you are on the right path, that you are where you need to be and that everything is happening perfectly as planned.

Go ahead! Take those baby steps each day toward your goal. You can do it, and you deserve it. Start creating the life you want.

Endnotes:

"Loving What Is: Four Questions That Can Change Your Life," by Byron Katie (Three Rivers Press).

"Codependent No More: How to Stop Controlling Others and Take Care of Yourself," by Melody Beattie (Hazelden).

Chapter Seven:
Suzanne Richardson

The Ripple Effect. What comes to mind when you hear that term? Throwing stones into a lake? Perhaps you can imagine that lake now, its glassy green surface surrounded by trees and not a soul besides yourself around for miles. Now picture the way a pebble might plunk into the water after you've thrown it in, causing uniform ripples to stream out toward the beach for a visual effect that lingers long after the rock has sunk invisibly to the bottom. What happens when you throw a large rock into the same lake? Or a handful of stones? A quiet riot ensues with big and small ripples intertwining and overlapping as they dance across the water's surface, insensible to the consequences they engender.

For Suzanne Richardson, these empirical facts form a metaphor by which she lives. The lake symbolizes our lives, and the stones are the people swimming in it. "We are all thrown into this big pond of life," she explains, "and each of us has an effect on one another. Some have a big effect and some have a little effect." In Suzanne's case, her husband, George, was one of those people who create a lot of ripples, both in her life and in the lives of those around them. Even today, long after he's passed away, Suzanne lives with the ripples he created and has found a way to transform them into a powerful optimism that motivates her in both work and life.

As we go through our lives, lessons and wisdom emerge in ways that we can use to help others, to create proverbial ripples, so to speak. The first time this idea was crystallized for Suzanne was when she was standing by George's grave site three weeks after he had passed. It was a beautiful, sunny day, and the adjacent road was buzzing with cars while Suzanne stood sobbing in the big, open field of the cemetery. She visited the grave weekly, and even though these trips made George's death more real for her, she took comfort in talking to him. That day, however, she was at a low point. Her body ached from mourning, she had no energy to look after her 7-year-old son, Robert, and she couldn't see how she'd be able to go on. She begged for some sign, some guidepost to tell her what to do. Suddenly she saw a huge, white tractor trailer coming down the road. Emblazoned on it were big letters that spelled "Robert." Stunned, she did a double-take and realized that God had responded and this was her answer: Robert was both her reason to move on, and the person she was supposed to help.

Slowly, Suzanne's epiphany began to unfold for her. She realized that she'd spent the last three weeks consumed by her loss and pain, which left little time to attend to the feelings of her son. People had assured her that it would get better, but she couldn't believe that as her body ached from the loss, and her heart felt as though it had just been ripped open. She thought to herself, How in the hell can this get better?

Now, however, she saw that she had been so wrapped up in self-pity while Robert was yearning for his dad's bedtime stories, their playtime together and his father's warmth and kind nature. Inspired by her husband's memory and spurred on by what she perceived as divine guidance, Suzanne began to fill in the gaps of George's absence by enrolling herself and Robert in bereavement groups. She realized they needed to deal with their grief appropriately, which meant having somebody there who could answer Robert's questions and support them both emotionally. She earnestly entered these groups looking for answers as she nurtured her mind, body and soul with meditation, healthy food and thankfulness.

A routine gradually emerged in which Suzanne would go to as many school activities as possible and make sure they had family dinners each night. She also returned to substitute teaching, which was a flexible job that let her spend much of her time with Robert. This predictability, along with a concerted effort to stay connected to each other emotionally, was vital to creating Suzanne and Robert's new family unit. It was also the way she could best focus on using her experience to help someone else and create more ripples of positivity in her son's life.

Suzanne's family life had always been defined by extreme, if unifying, experiences. She grew up with four sisters and one brother in Philadelphia during the 1960s, and hers was the kind of situation where space and money were so tight that Suzanne slept in an open drawer for the first few months of her life. Her parents never finished high school — they grew up during the Great Depression and had to go to work early on — but they had a worldly wisdom that they instilled in their children. Namely, they believed that by practicing courage and consistency you could make a good life for yourself. This was a lesson that would guide Suzanne later in life.

First, however, she ventured off to college to earn a teaching degree. This was a time when she began to turn away from the straitlaced lessons of her childhood in favor of a freer lifestyle. So when a mutual friend introduced her to George — an upbeat, optimistic boy who didn't party — the result was surprising. It was, she recalls, love at first sight. On their very first date, George declared, "I am going to marry you!" Time proved him right and, on September 18, 1981, they wed.

Though Suzanne and George seemed to be polar opposites, the fact was they shared an inner outlook that centered on gratitude and helping others. Many times we look at our lives and see only what's missing, but Suzanne's parents had taught her to appreciate what she had, and George felt the same way. They both recognized the value of the love and respect they felt for one another, and they rightly considered themselves lucky to have it.

But married life would be far from easy. It turned out that George suffered from hemophilia, a blood disorder that prevents clotting. As a result, George spent much of his life on the sidelines. "George could never play sports or ride a bike or drink alcohol," Suzanne explains, "and it was tough for him sitting on the porch watching others do it. If he got injured, he would have to go to the hospital right away because of the potential for a bleed-out."

The ways George's illness would impact their marriage appeared early on. As they made their way home from their honeymoon in Nova Scotia, the couple embarked on a ferry from Yarmouth to Portland, Maine. Enjoying the ride in the sunshine, they suddenly felt a jolt, and the ferry veered to the side. George accidentally hit his knee against something, and his knee joint began to bleed. Suzanne called the staff to get an ambulance. This was routine for George, and he reassured Suzanne he would be okay. He just needed ice to stop the bleeding.

But the people at the Portland hospital weren't equipped to deal adequately with his disease. Frustrated, Suzanne spent 10 hours making the normally an eight-hour trip back to Philadelphia, stopping frequently for ice to curb the bleeding. Throughout the ordeal, Suzanne just kept praying that George would be okay. She didn't have the luxury of being hysterical; she knew she had to stay positive. This was in God's hands.

Over the years, Suzanne came to rely on her faith in God and her grateful nature — not to mention the courage and consistency drilled into her by her parents — as she coped with George's illness. A turning point for her came on the night of a family activity at Robert's school, which George couldn't attend because he was all iced up and in pain. That night, Suzanne made a choice to look at the glass half-full. So many other fathers were absent because of work commitments, and she knew that if George could've made it, he would.

But pain and constant risk of injury were just the beginning of what George and Suzanne would have to endure. Two years after they married, news was released that the AIDS virus was in the clotting factor that her husband neededto survive. Nobody knew George was taking this tainted factor for several months in the '80s, but in 1983, as the newlyweds began to contemplate having children, they received the devastating news that George was HIV positive. At the time, they were overwhelmed with questions. What was this disease? What would be the effects on his hemophilia? Would George develop full-blown AIDS? Would Suzanne contract it too? Would it be possible to have children?

Suzanne has never been a religious person, but she is a spiritual person. If it weren't for her love for God, she doesn't believe she would've survived that horrible, potentially catastrophic discovery. "I would say, 'God, you got me in this situation, so you better help me out! Don't you leave me here, because I need help,'" Suzanne recalls. She could've focused on anger that this was happening, but all she felt was compassion for her husband and for others in the same situation. And she made a conscious effort to be grateful for the loving relationship she had despite all the hardships that arose from living with a terminal disease. She couldn't change the fact that George was ill, and it didn't make sense to her to waste her time with anger when she had precious little time left to spend with her husband.

At this point, George and Suzanne tried to live their lives to the fullest. George's accounting firm, which he'd started in 1981, grew more and more successful. Suzanne, meanwhile, worked as a substitute teacher for special-needs children. Perhaps it was this constant exposure to children, or perhaps it was because she knew she didn't have an endless future with her husband, but Suzanne yearned for children of her own. After years of thinking about it and discussing the pros and cons of having a child with an HIV-positive husband, something deep inside Suzanne told her it was time. She gave it over to God and, miraculously, she gave birth in November 1987 to a beautiful, healthy, HIV-free baby boy. They named him Robert. To this day, she and Robert continue to be HIV-free.

After 13 years of a loving marriage, George passed away from a gastrointestinal bleed, but Suzanne continues to feel nothing but gratitude for the time they had together. She gained so much courage and strength from her husband. She watched him face down his disease to live his life to the fullest, to build a business and make a marriage, to raise a son, to make them laugh and to encourage their family and friends to reach their goals.

George's courage and determination had a profound effect on all whose lives he touched. Robert, his son, is perhaps the most obvious example in that he is a biological extension of George. But he retains some of the same personal characteristics that defined his father. An accomplished chef, he practices gratitude in his daily life and looks to be a positive, uplifting pillar of hope for the people around him. Like his father, he tries to support his friends and colleagues when they're hurting, to find the good in every situation and to discover how they and he can use their experiences as learning opportunities or to help others.

For Suzanne, teaching alone couldn't fill the void after George passed away. Because she also loves to cook, she began to think about how she could use that to pay forward what she viewed as a great debt of good fortune in having been married to George. She went back to school to become a chef and today creates meals for an organization called Aid for Friends, which provides free, home-cooked meals primarily to elderly people who can't leave their homes. By living out her belief that you can take your experiences and use them to help others, she has attracted volunteers who deliver the meals she makes. Her meals and her volunteers are rippling throughout the Philadelphia area, showering the less fortunate with hope, encouragement and determination to stay strong.

Reflections

Life is often compared to a roller coaster of ups and downs and for good reason. And while most of us are anxious to speed through the low points of our lives, the focus, according to Suzanne's example, shouldn't necessarily be to get more positive experiences. It should be to understand how our interconnectedness shapes and defines our lives. Think about the following questions:

What would our lives be like if, instead of avoiding or dreading difficult times, we followed George and Suzanne's example and looked at those periods as learning experiences whose lessons we would eventually use to support and help others?

_____

_____

_____

Who would you be now?

_____

_____

Which person or people have had a profound effect on you?

_____

_____

_____

What have they taught you, and how can you use those lessons elsewhere in your life?

_____

_____

_____

_____

Where in your life are you developing a Ripple Effect on others? What does that feel like for you?

_____

_____

_____

_____

5. What impact can you create by turning your good and bad experiences into wisdom or actions that help someone else? What can you bring forth in others?

_____

_____

_____

_____

Chapter Eight:
Mary Sheila

Mary Sheila knew, as she sat curled up on the bathroom floor, that her life could not continue this way. She was four-months pregnant and cowering in the bathroom as her drunk, high and angry husband, Joe, banged on the door and screamed that she was a bitch. She knew that if he got into the bathroom or if she came out, she would suffer a night of physical and sexual abuse. This was the norm when he came home from a drinking binge — the yelling, the profanity and the sex. Sitting in the bathroom, shaking and crying quietly in fear, she thought to herself, This is sick. What am I doing? I have to get out of this situation. Suddenly it was quiet. Had Joe passed out, leaving her free to emerge from her safe house? As she got up from the floor, she heard a little voice in her head say, "It is time for you to leave." So she opened the door, stepped over her unconscious husband who was crumpled on the floor, packed a bag and left for good.

Mary, a 5-foot-4 brunet beauty with a big smile, had married her high-school sweetheart in 1978. She did so against the wishes of her father, who knew Joe for what he was: an abusive alcoholic. Mary, however, figured Joe was the best she could get. She had seen the highs and lows of alcoholism in her own family, but she believed that Joe would change. Her first wake-up call to reality, however, was on her wedding day when Joe showed up drunk and stoned.

As a practicing Catholic, Mary considered her wedding day to be the most important day of her life. She wanted the ceremony to be perfect, and with all her family and friends in attendance she couldn't back out at the last minute, so she put on a smile and pretended everything was okay. But as she walked down the aisle, she thought, Gee, Mary, what are you thinking? It was the same voice of reason that, much later, would compel her to leave her husband. That day, however, she ignored it. Dying inside of shame and embarrassment, and swimming in denial, Mary took her vows. She had grown up surrounded by addicts and, as a result, became the person who would make things look better to the outside world. But could she do that in her marriage?

Eighteen months into it, Mary became pregnant. She and Joe had spent a good portion of that time trying to conceive and participating in fertility and potency tests, so Mary came to believe this baby was the answer to her marriage's problems. She had seen how her own mother kept having kids in an effort to fix their dysfunctional family situation. Eventually Mary's father did get sober, and Mary hoped this baby would inspire the same change in Joe.

In Mary's marriage, however, physical and emotional abuse ran rampant, especially when Joe was drunk. Earlier in the pregnancy, when she was so nauseated with morning sickness that she couldn't get out of bed, Joe came home with one of his hangovers and said, "Get the hell out of bed and make me something to eat." Somehow, Mary got up to make scrambled eggs but became violently ill and threw up on the floor. Joe started yelling at her because he was really hungry, and she wasn't making the eggs fast enough. Mary knew this scenario was wrong, but she convinced herself that she just had to get through the pregnancy and then everything would change for the better.

But the drinking and drug abuse continued, and Mary's family and friends grew increasingly concerned over her situation. Joe was using marijuana and heroin, and he was controlling and manipulative with Mary. As she heard the disappointment in her parents' voices, she began to realize her situation was a potentially harmful one in which to raise a baby. Not only was she desperately unhappy; her home was emotionally unhealthy for her, Joe and any baby she might have.

Then that night arrived when she was four months pregnant and scared enough to leave Joe for good. After she'd left, she'd only return to the apartment when she needed something and could have her brothers and sister accompany her. Finally, her siblings told Joe to move out. He responded by taking jewelry and furniture, grinding cat excrement into the carpet and moving in with his new girlfriend.

Mary, who was living with her parents, waited two weeks. Finally, she felt confident that Joe wouldn't harm her anymore or return to their home, which was actually a refurbished chicken coop. (The ceiling was no higher than 5 feet, 5 inches but the place had a bathroom, bedroom, living room and kitchen.) When Mary did come home, she discovered that, spitefully, Joe had not cleaned the litter boxes for at least three weeks, and there were cat feces all over the apartment. Because cat feces can be dangerous to pregnant women, Mary was both frightened and devastated. If Joe could do this to cats and to her, what else was he capable of doing?

She would soon find out. After she settled back in, Joe would come around late at night, entering the first-floor apartment through the windows and scaring her. He'd push her around, and they would fight so loudly the neighbors would intervene and even referee. Finally, Mary changed the locks and told the police and her neighbors to keep an eye out if her husband were around. Feeling defeated that Joe hadn't and wouldn't change, she conceded to put up with occasional disturbances so long as she didn't have to be married to him anymore.

At this point, Mary was unemployed and on Medicaid, which is how she gave birth to her baby boy, Scott, in April of 1980. Mary stayed with her parents for just three weeks after delivering, and then she returned home to a staggeringly difficult existence. Joe couldn't be pinned down to provide child support, and he was unemployed anyway, so Mary had to sign up for welfare. At most, she'd receive $40 a month, so she supplemented her income by cleaning houses, a job that allowed her to bring her baby with her.

Mary's reality was harsh: She had no real job to speak of, no money and no father for her child. Yet she knew deep in her soul that God was going to take care of her somehow, and she trusted God implicitly. She also had the unconditional support of her family, who continued to love her and help when and how they could, like by providing free meals and groceries. Mary's mother, for example, came by one day on her way home from church. While they were chatting, her mother opened the refrigerator and found no food, just bags of breast milk. In her kind and supportive way, Mary's mom said, "How about coming over for dinner?" Mary accepted and, as she was leaving, her mom sent her home with bags of groceries.

But what differentiates Mary's story from so many other people's, what helped her to move forward instead of sinking into social and financial oblivion, was her commitment to her faith in God. Because she knew He would provide for her, she unquestioningly set herself to the tasks before her. For example, Mary had to get divorced and obtain Medicaid in order to have her child. She also had to sign up for food stamps and a federally funded program known as the Women, Infants and Children (WIC) Nutrition Program, which provides nutritious food to low-income women and children. These were necessary steps, but for Mary, they were excruciatingly embarrassing. She would routinely walk across the street to the grocery store at 11:30 p.m. just so she wouldn't risk being seen by anyone she knew as she shopped with her food stamps and WIC aid.

Despite all this, Mary remained positive, convinced there was a divine strength burning inside her heart. She prayed, and she felt a new self-awareness, a conviction she could succeed in life, which she read as divine responses to her prayers. This strength or, as Mary puts it, grace, inspired her to take actions she had always been too scared to try before. She'd wanted a life free from fear, and so she left her husband. She realized she might always be a single parent — a terrifying prospect for someone with codependent tendencies — but she was unhesitating in her acceptance of that. And, perhaps most significantly, she realized that to be a good parent she had to figure out how to take care of both herself and Scott.

When she had been married to Joe, Mary had taken a certification course to become an aide for the Visiting Nurse Association (VNA). After her divorce, she moved into private duty nursing, and then she began to work in hospice for the VNA. Eventually, Mary remarried and began to take evening classes in her community college's Health and Physical Education program.

Mary was now empowered and ambitious, and she didn't stop with just one career. To date, she has certifications as a Pilates instructor (both on the Mat and the Reformer), an aerobics instructor and a personal trainer. She also owns a nutritional-supplement business and is the landlord of three apartments.

Thirty-one years have passed since those dark days of Mary's first marriage. She is happily remarried with four children by her second husband and two grandchildren from Scott, who remains an integral part of her life. Because Joe is also involved in Scott's life, Mary sees him occasionally at family functions. But Mary, who says it's like that part of her life never happened, has forgiven both herself and Joe.

Because of the things Mary has survived and done, she has a fuller understanding of who she is and what she wants. When she was a child, she never opened her mouth because the addicts in her life created chaos and got all the attention. Now that she is living the life she chose and made happen, she is her true self: gregarious, charismatic, outgoing and opinionated. And, most importantly, she is no longer afraid — of a husband, of possibilities or of life.

Reflections

Mary Sheila views her first marriage and its aftermath as opportunities for growth, so she is in a distinct position to encourage others not to repeat her mistakes. Don't, she tells people, settle in a relationship by thinking, This is the best that it can be. Find the person who shares your beliefs, goals and faith, she says. You have to connect with like minded people.

When any of us examine our relationships, Mary suggests we ask ourselves these questions and answer them with strict honesty:

What positive attributes does a friend/mate bring to your relationship?

_____

_____

_____

_____

What must you have in your relationships that can't be compromised?

_____

_____

_____

_____

How are you going to get that? What would it look like?

_____

_____

_____

_____

What role does faith play in your relationship?

_____

_____

_____

In what ways can you open yourself up to the paths presented by a higher power?

_____

_____

_____

_____

Where in your life have you tried to be in control? What happened, and was it the result you wanted?

_____

_____

_____

It is okay to remember that you cannot change somebody unless she/he wants to change him/herself. Many times when we let go, Mary notes, the outcomes are better than we ever imagined.

Ultimately, Mary has learned that we must surround ourselves with people who make our own life stories better. We are not meant to live on this earth alone. Who can help you make your life story better?

Endnote:

Consultation with Joni Bury, MEd, CPCC; The Dream Network.

Chapter Nine:
Amy Stevens

What would you do if you knew you could not fail? For many of us, the answer to this question depends on circumstances like timing and finances. But what if we instead approached our lives with the confidence that we would be okay no matter what life threw at us? What if we looked at failure as an opportunity to learn instead of a reason to give up? Amy Stevens chose to live this way. She looked fear in the eye and said, "I can handle whatever happens to me and be okay."

Life would put her conviction to the test. In June 1997, Amy and her husband, Gus, were designing their dream home in Pennsylvania and raising their son, Matthew, when they were hit with the news that a recurring melanoma had metastasized to Gus' brain. Suddenly Amy's life turned upside down. She spent an agonizing five weeks watching the love of her life suffer and decline before passing away in August. Memories of the 12 years they had together — not to mention their plans for the future and the house they were building — overwhelmed her with emotion.

Amid her depression and bewilderment, 32-year-old Amy faced an uncertain future. The row house in Roxborough, Philadelphia that she, Gus and Matthew once filled with laughter and love now felt like an empty shell. And as she took a month off from her position as a litigation paralegal to mourn, she began to realize that living in Roxborough was no longer ideal for her and Matthew. Gus' family lived close by, but their visits had become stressful. Amy had her own ideas about how she wanted to raise Matthew and move on, and these were often at odds with her mother-in-law's plans. Finally, needing breathing room and a fresh start, Amy decided to move.

On one hand, Amy's move was true to character. She had always been a strong-willed person, and an overbearing mother-in-law was an obvious catalyst. On the other hand, Amy didn't exactly strike out on her own — she moved back in with her parents in northeastern Philadelphia. But returning to the nest was a calculated move: Amy's main concern was for her 6-year-old son's emotional stability, which her parents could provide, especially when she returned to work. The move also bought her time to contemplate bigger questions. How would she make ends meet? What would become of them? How could she go on without Gus?

Amy answered these questions over the next 13 months by essentially reorganizing her life. She decided that she needed to sell the house in Roxborough, which harbored too many memories, and move someplace new. She put a deposit down on a townhouse that fit the bill and, in September 1998, she and Matthew moved in.

At this point, Amy's world looked vastly different than it had the previous year. She had a new house and, after struggling with familial disapproval, she'd even started dating again. She missed her husband, but she also missed having a partner and a father for her son. Even so, she wasn't expecting to hit it off the way she did with Joe, the man she met on a blind date and whom she would go on to marry in 2002.

Sometimes people lose themselves in projects in order to avoid processing grief. For Amy, however, organizing was cathartic. Her world had spun out of control, so she regained control where she could: in her home and in her romantic life.

Amy's professional life, however, presented ongoing challenges. Despite making frequent reports to her superiors, Amy endured a colleague's sexual harassment for a year. Finally, in October 2003, Amy decided self-respect trumped employment, and she resigned from the legal firm where she worked without so much as a two-week notice.

In retrospect, Amy views this experience as a gift, because it forced her to make a decision that ultimately led to a more fulfilling career. In order to get there, however, she had to engage in the sort of soul-searching that necessarily precedes overhauling your life. She asked herself questions like, What is your purpose in life? What is important to you? Who do you need to be in order to create a fulfilling life? As she went round and round these subjects in her head, she kept hearing a little voice telling her she needed to start her own business. But how? What could she do that would capitalize on her knowledge and experiences and still be the sort of job she'd want to do every day?

The answer took a surprising form: a television show called Mission: Organization on HGTV, which demonstrates, one room at a time, the nuts and bolts of how to create order out of chaos. For Amy, the magic was in watching the ways organizing a home translated to empowerment in people's lives. This, Amy suddenly realized, was her calling.

Sure, her background was in law, but she also had life experience and a knack for organizing — not to mention a healthy dose of chutzpah. Now she also had a vision.

Amy has always believed that anything is possible, but she also knew that you must be open to what the world offers, you must have passion and perseverance and you must draw on your life experiences. In her own life, Amy tenaciously tackled her vision and made time to work on it every day. She found mentors to help guide her, and she maintained faith it would work out no matter what came her way. Amy eventually grew so passionate about researching how to start her own residential-organization business that she was willing to risk not having a steady income. Joe, however, was feeling the pressure of being a sole provider. He wanted to be supportive and believed she should leave her old job where she was suffering harassment. But he couldn't understand why Amy would start a business in an entirely new industry instead of finding a job at a different law firm where she would be well-compensated. Eventually, his doubt and other factors took a toll on their marriage, and they divorced in 2009.

Amy, however, knew what she was doing. Thanks to her experience as a paralegal, she had developed a solid business background. She knew how to create contracts and proposals, she knew which questions to ask clients and she knew how to run a business, what marketing to pursue, how to network and how to handle billing. So in a way, Amy was already primed to start her own company. The other part of it — the organizing — had to be fine-tuned. So over the next six months, Amy did her homework. She sought out other professional organizers to understand how they operated their businesses. She reviewed their websites to see what services they offered and what their price structures were like. She went on line and researched home-organization principles and what kinds of materials people used. She borrowed library books that covered residential organization. She hired a business coach to inspire and challenge her to stay on task, to set goals and to simultaneously support her and hold her accountable as she moved forward. She listened to webinars and telecasts on how to organize, how to market yourself and how to keep up with social media. She was busier than ever, but she was also happier than ever.

Amy had learned early on to trust her instincts — they were, after all, what drove her to approach Gus the first time she saw him across the room. They were what drove her to quit her job and start her own company. And today she continues to honor that intuition by refusing to compromise what she believes in, whether it is with family or with her career. Her single-minded focus and unwavering commitment have propelled Amy into a profession that is both fulfilling and empowering to those she helps. Every woman, she explains, needs a sense of self. Wherever she might be in her life is simply a stepping stone, Amy says, to her future.

By defying the odds and popular opinion, Amy managed to build a lucrative business that continues to support herself and her 21-year-old son. This alone was worth the effort, and it is one of many reasons why, when business slows down, she never regrets her decision to follow her dream. She loves empowering women through organization. And, most of all, she appreciates the power, the beauty and the symmetry of transforming rooms the way she transformed her own life.

Reflections

By trusting her instincts and pursuing her goals with relentless passion, Amy Stevens created the profession and life she wanted. She took the time to sift through what she had done and been in her past, she listened to the people who knew her best and she settled on a course of action to achieve her goals. She had a vision of where she wanted to go, and she never looked back.

Do you know where you're going? Do you like the road you're traveling? It's time to take an inventory of your life.

Consider your career, health, relationships and finances as you answer the following questions to create a plan for the life you desire.

Where do you want to be? (What is your desired outcome?)

_____

_____

_____

_____

What measurement will tell you when you have achieved your goal? (Dates on a calendar, inches lost, miles run, book written, move or advancement achieved?)

_____

_____

_____

_____

_____

_____

Where are you now? (What issues or challenges are you facing?)

_____

_____

_____

_____

_____

How do you get there? What action steps do you need to take in order to close the gap between your present and your future? How can you keep these plans flexible enough to achieve your desired outcome?

_____

_____

_____

_____

_____

What changes may happen in the next one to five years that may affect your outcome?

_____

_____

_____

_____

_____

As you create and implement your plan, be sure to schedule an appointment with yourself each day to work toward that vision. You can accomplish anything when you have confidence and clarity in your mission and faith in something greater than yourself.

Sherry Shoemaker

Chapter Ten:
Dawn Rieder

Energetic, bubbly, bright, tremendously determined and organized — these are just a handful of characteristics embodied by Dawn Rieder who is the kind of woman many of us aspire to be. Whether as a teacher or a mother, Dawn never stops setting and meeting her goals, so when she decided to return to work in 2003 after staying home with her 5- and 7-year-old kids, she saw only good things ahead of her.

But Dawn never got past the stage of dusting off her résumé and filling out applications. Instead of scheduling interviews, she found herself curled up on the sofa, exhausted, achy and frustrated. How, she asked herself, could she be so lazy and irresponsible about something she wanted so badly? She loved being a mom, and staying at home wasn't strenuous, so why couldn't she get off the couch? Could she be depressed without knowing it?

Disgusted with the endless fatigue and achiness, Dawn visited her family doctor who told her not to work out for three to four weeks and see what happened. When she got worse, Dawn knew there had to be something physically wrong, so she returned to her doctor and demanded blood work. After an autoimmune panel, X-rays and an MRI scan, the doctor found a lot of arthritis for a 36-year-old woman, but the cause was unclear, so Dawn had to wait another week for more test results.

Around this time, Dawn's husband planned a trip to Florida for business and as a quick getaway for him and his wife. It was a chance for Dawn to relax and spend time alone with her husband and not think about her medical issues. But even though she was careful to stay out of the sun, red lesions erupted all over her body as the weekend progressed. She called her doctor from Florida, and his response was far from comforting. He told her she needed to come to the office as soon as she returned home. When her doctor saw her lesions, he informed her that she had lupus, an auto-immune disease that results in inflammation and damage to the joints, skin and blood vessels throughout the body.

Dawn was in shock. Her first thought was, At least it's not cancer. She had never heard of lupus, so how bad could it be? It only took one internet search and an afternoon at the library for her to change her mind. Sobbing, Dawn decided that maybe death from cancer would be better.

Immediately, Dawn's thoughts turned to her husband and children, the family who would ultimately rally behind her. How do you tell a 5- and 7-year-old that you are dying? Who would take care of her children after she was gone? And while she was alive, how would she cope with the pain she was told to expect on a daily basis? How were she and her husband supposed to "accept" this? They had plans for their future; there were so many things they wanted to do together and with their daughters.

Outraged that her kids and husband hadn't asked for this but were stuck with it anyway, Dawn became determined to change their situation. This disease, she decided, was unacceptable. Dying was simply not an option for her.

So Dawn tapped the perseverance that she'd always relied

on to meet her life's goals. She searched out the best rheumatologist, the first step in coordinating care, and eventually figured out how to engage the team of specialists her complicated case required. By the time she met with the right rheumatologist, her symptoms had multiplied. She lost feeling in one leg and suffered incontinence, migraines, fainting, digestive and swallowing issues and a racing heartbeat. The lupus had begun to attack her autonomic system, which meant that all the functions it oversees, like breathing and heartbeat, were at risk. In fact, Dawn would go on to suffer a stroke and vasculitis (an inflammation of the blood vessels), which would relegate her to a wheelchair for three months.

Along with the physical reality came a jarring mental and emotional landscape. Dawn's doctor at the University of Pennsylvania told her that she had three to five years to live and was essentially a "walking time bomb" who should live her life while she had it. Her heart could stop beating or her lungs could stop functioning at any time. This was her new reality, and she had to come to terms with it.

Perhaps not surprisingly, Dawn grappled with her faith, asking that age-old question of how a kind and loving God could permit such suffering. Yet, when she looked, there were blessings all around her. She struggled on good days to exert a minimum effort so as to preserve her strength. On bad days, she would be bedridden or hospitalized, but neighbors would unexpectedly show up with meals or help coordinate carpools for Dawn's daughters. And the greatest gift was the way her family grew closer. Now there was more laughter. The little things that had bothered them before didn't really seem to matter anymore. Their collective focus became spending time together. (They even built a vacation home where they can have fun and relax.) Perhaps the most poignant example of her renewed commitment to her family is the way Dawn tucks her daughters into bed every night, unsure of what tomorrow may bring.

Throughout her disease, Dawn has felt compelled to keep her daughters informed about what happens, and their response has been overwhelming. They have eagerly shouldered basic household chores like laundry and cleaning alongside skills more specific to Dawn's situation, like learning how to work a wheelchair. They have all gone to therapy as a family to help them work through the questions and fear that accompany living with a terminal disease. Dawn's husband — who would stay home as Dawn needed him — and her girls have always wanted to do whatever they could to help keep her alive, even when that meant asking Santa for a Christmas gift of Mommy getting better. Her family, in other words, has become her support system and renews her strength after a bad day.

Just as important as letting those in her life help her has been Dawn's commitment to finding a purpose for each of her days. For Dawn, purpose is twofold. On one hand, she works to be fully present for her family and friends. On the other, she helps people who have the same debilitating disease. As Dawn puts it, "Either you laugh or you cry under these circumstances, and I'd rather laugh." So despite her daily pain, Dawn trained in 2009 to become a leader of the Lupus Foundation of America's tri-state chapter and raise money for research. Dawn's work with the organization is varied. She participates in group discussions with other patients, provides medical and informational resources and even coordinates details like meals and birthday cards to patients who need moral support.

Dawn took her commitments even further when she and her family decided to do the Lupus Loop, a fundraising walk. They beat their goal of raising $1,000 in one day to ultimately raise $10,000 that year. Since that first walk, Dawn and her family have continued to walk every year after (as Dawn's health allows), and each time they raise more money than the previous year. It has become both fun and addictive, and it has contributed to Dawn's sense of purpose.

In a way, Dawn's fundraising efforts are a natural evolution from her work with her church. For the past five years, she has regularly organized popular women's teas — replete with a fashion show and guest speaker — as part of her church's evangelic outreach. In 2011, it occurred to her that if these events worked at church, they could also work to raise money for lupus. She was ready for a change from the walks, and this could be something where her formidable organizational skills might reap a significant financial advantage. (After all, she says, she has no control over her illness, but she does have control over fund raisers and her attitude.) The result was a dessert party and fashion show that drew a crowd of more than 300 to raise more than $8,000.

By harnessing her energy and pouring it into her purpose-filled goals, and by relying on her family's support and her medical team's expertise, Dawn has not only defied the odds, she's made everyone around her happier. It has been perhaps the biggest surprise of her illness: Allowing others to do little things for her, like running the vacuum or going to the grocery store, gives them a sense of purpose that they find fulfilling. It is often the equivalent of what the Lupus Loop and fund raisers are to her.

Eight years after her diagnosis, Dawn is still going strong. She has good days and bad days, but her sense of purpose and attitude are a big part of what continues to keep her alive in every sense of the word.

Reflections

Dawn has found her sense of purpose in the way she lives with lupus. By focusing on areas in her life where she has control, she's discovered her passion for helping others. In this way, she is not unusual. Many times it takes a disastrous event for someone to find her purpose because it forces her to clarify how to live life intentionally. You, however, don't have to wait for tragedy to strike. Take a look at your life now, and make a list of the good, the bad and the ugly. Ask yourself the following:

Where in your life are you making a unique contribution to family or friends?

_____

_____

_____

_____

_____

What difference are you making in your life and in the lives of others?

_____

_____

_____

_____

Where in your life are you willing to share your story to help others grow?

_____

_____

_____

_____

What is the teaching that you are called to do?

_____

_____

_____

_____

In order for you to answer your calling, what must you say "yes" to in your life, and what must you say "no" to? For Dawn, she must answer "yes" to helping others with lupus; she must say "no" to thinking every day that she's going to die.

_____

_____

_____

_____

Chapter Eleven:
Nancy Venner

Throughout our lives, we will encounter many challenges, from a job loss or divorce, to perhaps abuse or even the death of a child. These challenges — or at least our responses to them — often come to define us. On one hand, we may choose to languish in despair, ruminating on why something terrible happened to us. (Or why we don't deserve it.) On the other hand, we may look at the situation and wonder, Why not me?

Okay, so maybe the second option isn't a common reaction. At best, many of us will suck it up and get through it; few of us will actually appreciate the bad stuff as it happens. But what if we did get to that next level of acceptance? What if we embraced challenges and heartache because they made us better? (Or at least gave us the ability to help other people feel better!) What if we really believed in our heart of hearts that there are no "bad" people; that those who do bad things to us do them out of desperation?

Well, if we adopted that kind of attitude, we'd have quite a bit in common with Nancy Venner, the petite, attractive, 50–something woman who lives according to these very principles. And her extraordinary story has tested and solidified those beliefs many times over.

For Nancy, the desire to help others was instilled in her at an early age. Her family was so active in their community that, instead of play dates and birthday parties, Nancy often spent her childhood weekends bringing gifts to kids in orphanages, doing walks for March of Dimes or going to nursing homes to visit the elderly. When Nancy asked her dad why they did so much for others, he described their work as "breaking down fences" for the people they helped. Sometimes, he explained, those fences were real and sometimes they were metaphorical, but the idea was to give under served people positive experiences they might not otherwise have.

The fence imagery resonated with Nancy. At the age of 10, she participated in her first fund raiser as a member of the Jaycees, an organization that encourages young people to get active in their communities. She spent so much of her childhood volunteering that it wasn't surprising when her chosen university — located in crime-ridden Northern Philadelphia — felt more like an opportunity to help than a reason to run the other way. Homelessness, for example, was rampant, and Nancy's reaction was to give food to those people on her way to school. She'd spent enough time with the homeless to know that most were inherently good people who were just stuck in a bad situation.

Still, her familiarity with homelessness didn't make her transition to university life easy. This was the 1980s, and at her particular school, some areas of campus intersected with fairly dangerous parts of town. Rundown housing projects rose up menacingly along the streets, while gang members and petty criminals seemed always to be on the prowl.

An experience on Nancy's first day at school set the tone for the rest of her college career. She was resting on a park bench when a professor told her to move for her own safety. But while she may have learned not to loiter in public spaces, she didn't learn to avoid the neighborhood. She usually ran late for class, and rather than waste time looking for a parking space in the full lots, she'd frequently park in the outlying neighborhood. As a result, she'd have to cut through the streets on foot to get to class on time.

Unfortunately, Nancy's routine presence in the neighborhood would have serious consequences. It started small. One day, on her way to her car, Nancy naively took out her wallet to buy lunch at a food vendor. In the blink of an eye, her wallet was snatched.

Another time, Nancy was driving with her window open and had her handbag on the passenger seat. Someone stopped her for the time and stole her purse! But this time, something clicked inside Nancy. Oblivious to the gangs and drug addicts around her, she ran after the thief. It was such a patently bad idea that even the bystanders knew better. Suddenly, a big, burly African-American man picked her up, swung her over his shoulder and said, "Where do you think you're going? You need to leave!" She screamed that somebody had her wallet, and he retorted, "You are going to get killed. Don't you see that you are the only white person in this neighborhood?" Suddenly Nancy realized the man was there to help her, and she let him take her to a pay phone to call the police. As she waited, a woman who was visibly intoxicated but who also radiated an essence of kindness approached her, ostensibly to help and give her money for a phone call. "What are you doing here?" she asked Nancy. "You don't belong here. I know you are going to be somebody someday." These two people — who stayed with her until the police arrived — were like her guardian angels.

Perhaps it was because of them that Nancy always felt protected; she knew there was always good around, even in bad circumstances. And their actions helped to underscore Nancy's faith in humanity.

The next few years, however, would challenge that faith. Nancy was the victim of a tremendous number of assaults and robberies. Yes, she went to school in a rough neighborhood, and yes, she lived fearlessly. But when something as simple as going to a baseball game could end in a robbery — someone grabbed her wallet while she paid for a hotdog — Nancy had to wonder why. But it wasn't until she was sexually assaulted that she began to actively look for a way to change things.

One day, when she went to work through her school-work program, a coworker started aggressively groping her in the mail room. Nancy courageously kicked and screamed and scratched her way out, but the incident left her feeling confused, frustrated and embarrassed. Suddenly, she began to ask herself the right questions about why this kept happening. Was it her demeanor? The way she walked or dressed? True, she always felt a divine protection, but she decided it was time to take an active role in protecting herself as well. She signed up for a self-defense class, which empowered her to learn how to walk with intention and to become more aware of her surroundings. She also engaged in counseling to mentally deal with what happened to her. Now she knew to avoid the people who looked shady by crossing the street or not making eye contact. She was determined not to be the victim anymore.

As much as Nancy didn't want to be a victim, she didn't want to be a bystander either. Too often, she believes, people are victimized while others passively look on. But with her father's words reverberating through her mind, Nancy renewed her commitment to getting people on the other side of the fence. This was her purpose, she felt, and as long as she was living that purpose, she intuited that God would continue to protect her. And her experiences with robbery and assault, she thought, were simply more avenues whereby she could understand and help others.

It didn't take long for Nancy to put these convictions into practice. One night, as she was walking to her car, she saw a girl sitting on a bench in an open lot near campus. She appeared completely unaware that a nearby group of guys was scoping out the gold chains around her neck. Nancy, who was standing across the street, yelled to the girl, trying to get her attention, but it was too late. The guys yanked the chains off her neck and ran. The girl started sobbing. "Please help!" she cried. "Those chains are my mom's!"

Without hesitation or fear, Nancy took off after the thieves, praying to God to protect her. She knew, suddenly, clearly, that she was there specifically to stop some of these assaults. And she was determined to fulfill her destiny.

Unfortunately, that destiny took her into a rundown housing project. She bravely entered the building to hunt down the guy who she believed had the jewelry. The stench of garbage and urine stung her nostrils. Rats scurried by as she climbed the stairs. Her heart was pounding out of her chest, and she thought, What am I doing here? Am I crazy to do this? God, please protect me! Finally she arrived, winded and sweaty, at the top of the stairs where the hallway was lined with door-less apartments. She pressed on through the narrow, dimly lit hallway and heard the culprit's voice bellow down the aisle, "If you can help me, I will give you the chains."

The commotion drew the residents out of their apartments and into the hallway with Nancy. They just stared at her. For Nancy, this was more unnerving than shouting. Would they kill her? Help her? Or simply watch indifferently as the spectacle unfolded? But her panic lasted only a few moments. Somehow sensing that God would protect her, Nancy's strength and determination returned.

On her way down the hall, a drunken woman emerged from an apartment and just stared at her. Beyond her in the apartment were the guys Nancy was chasing! She ignored the roaches crawling over piles of pizza and watermelon, because the boys who took the chains were there — and they were jeering and laughing at her! "You told me you had the chains!" Nancy furiously shouted at them before grabbing the person who she believed was the ringleader. With divine bravery, she held him in hand and told him he was going to jail. To her surprise, the neighbors surrounded her and agreed with her. They even helped Nancy escort him out of the building and into police custody!

She never got the chains — a fact made all the worse when Nancy found out the girl's mother had passed away — but she did succeed in a different way. She testified against the man she helped arrest, partly because it was the right thing to do, and partly because she had to prove him wrong. As she visited him in jail, she asked him why he'd chosen this path. He replied, "Did you see where I live? Did you see that woman? She was my mother. Nothing will change for me."

The way Nancy saw it, things had already changed for him. His situation was heartbreaking, but Nancy believed — and told him so — that he had the power to change his life. And with his arrest acting as a pause button on the destructive path he'd previously chosen, he could seize the opportunity to make a new, more productive life for himself.

Getting people to the other side of that fence has become Nancy's life's work. She decided somewhere between pursuing attackers and defending victims that she was going to be what nobody else wanted to be: The person who stands up against wrongdoing and makes a positive impact on other people's lives. Nancy has been able to do this on several levels. Professionally, she's developed a career in the nonprofit sector; and personally, she continues to fortify her commitment to help others via her faith, therapy and experiences. And her outlook on life remains as indomitable as ever. As she sees it, "There are no bad days; just character-building ones."

Reflections

It may be difficult at times for us to find the good in bad situations, but accepting that such experiences are simply ours to bear can change our perspective from that of a victim to that of a conqueror. If we can honestly evaluate our situation, no matter how horrific, and try to find the gift tucked in it rather than play the role of its victim, we may discover hidden opportunities to help either ourselves or others.

Difficult times are also chances to hone our convictions and, sometimes, to take a stand for what we believe in. Perhaps we must do something as basic as tell the truth. Or maybe we're required to accomplish something more complicated, like stand by our values regarding what's right and wrong. The idea in any scenario is not to compromise the good we must achieve. This is a concept thoughtfully outlined by Ron Renaud in his book, "The Uncompromised."

So how can you be the example others want to emulate? The following are some questions to help you fine-tune your own value system. By thoughtfully understanding your values, you can have a clearer sense of how to put them into practice. This, to paraphrase Gandhi, allows you ultimately to become the change you want to see in the world.

What do you believe is good?

_____

_____

_____

What is not acceptable to you in your life right now?
What are you willing to do about it?

_____

_____

_____

What are your spiritual beliefs? Are you willing to follow
them? Why?

_____

_____

_____

What impact do you want to make in the world around
you? What changes must you make in your life in order
for that to happen?

_____

_____

_____

What is important to you in your life? What will it take
to stand firmly in your beliefs?

_____

_____

_____

_____

How do you want to be perceived, both at work and at home? Why?

_____

_____

_____

What legacy do you want to leave for others? Why?

_____

_____

_____

Where in your life are you compromising your beliefs? Where are you standing firm? Why?

_____

_____

_____

Endnote:

"The Uncompromised," by Ron Renaud (Washington Franklin Publishing Paperback, 2011).

Chapter 12:

Sherry Shoemaker

Hi! I am Sherry Shoemaker — do you like me? Am I good enough, pretty enough and smart enough for you? Am I coming across too strong? Don't worry; I can change that! I can be anything you want me to be!

Believe it or not, this introduction sums up how I used to approach relationships in my life. Sure, I wasn't quite so obvious, but the desperate, do-anything-to-please attitude was definitely there. I was a chameleon and a people-pleaser. I was always striving to be perfect. (But at what cost?) I was always ready with contingency plans in case something didn't work out. (But to protect whom?) I thought I could keep all the balls up in the air and, sometimes, it worked. But the price was high: I had anxiety, guilt and depression; I lived in constant fear of failure; I was overly controlling and prone to nagging. How did I end up that way?

As a young child, I was sickly and bullied by my classmates for not being able to participate in activities. (Even simple things like rolling on the grass were off-limits because I was so allergic.) But that was only the half of it. The disease of alcoholism had infected my family, and its seeds of codependency, like needing to control others and fix things for them, had taken root in every area of my life. Of course, the day-to-day stuff was bad, too. Discipline ruled our house, and if I broke the rules, I was punished severely. It might have been yelling, it might have been hitting or it might have been beatings. As a result, I was always on alert and never knew what I was coming home to. Many days I found solace in my bedroom, playing alone in the woods or on the playground with other kids. At these places, I could be myself and express my feelings without fear that they were somehow wrong.

By the time I hit middle and high school, I had come out of my cocoon and blossomed into a social butterfly. I participated in many school activities, from marching band to tennis, and I discovered that boys were attracted to me, because I was pretty and smart and capable of doing a lot more than I knew. Just to tick off my parents, I would accomplish things they told me I couldn't do. But while it was rewarding to prove them wrong, I still suffered from guilt because, at the heart of it, I so wanted to please them and earn positive recognition.

The drive to be perfect and not disappoint others lasted all through high school and into my adulthood. That, of course, took its toll. I strived for good grades and perfect body image, which led me to bulimia in my early 20s and then therapy, where I soon realized that my feelings did in fact matter.

But fear overrode that realization. I was terrified of being abandoned, and I wanted to be liked and to matter so badly that I was needy in relationships. Those relationships never lasted more than a year, and when they inevitably ended, I would replay each scenario over and over in my head, thinking how, if I'd done or said something differently, things might have worked out. The men I attracted, meanwhile, were fun-loving but also alcoholic, self-centered and egotistic — and I was the perfect enabler.

As I approached my mid-20s after a traumatic breakup, I was gradually improving my self-esteem with therapy. I'd been living on my own since I was 21 and was working as a teacher while also taking on part-time restaurant work, so I was very self-sufficient. It was then, at the age of 26, that I met my husband. He was the handsomest man I'd ever seen, and he had a great position working in sales for a small company. When we met, it was love at first sight. He was everything I wanted in a man: caring, loved to party, adventurous and funny. We could talk about everything and anything. Within a year we were engaged, and we married in July of 1982. Our lives were blissful, and during the first year of our marriage, I became pregnant. My husband was, I knew, my knight in shining armor.

We were blessed with the birth of our first son, who was so adorable with his big blue eyes and blonde hair. I was excited, I was in awe and then, after a week of help from my husband and mom, I was on my own. My mom went back home, and my husband, who was climbing the corporate ladder, traveled extensively. That left me in uncharted territory as a new mom with a colicky child and limited support. Yet all those old drives to be perfect kicked in, so I channeled my insecurity into my child, myself and my home. The house had to be perfect, I had to look perfect and, outwardly, we did appear pretty perfect. But inside, I was so lonely and resentful that my husband was only around on weekends to help, and I was so insecure, that I became overprotective, exhausted and, in short, a nagging bitch. My husband and I, not surprisingly, fought constantly.

As time passed, I became pregnant with my second child, and God granted us a beautiful baby girl. Within six months, we found ourselves moving to corporate headquarters in Montreal, Canada with a 2-year-old and a 6-month-old. Culture shock hit me hard — this was my first move away from home (outside of college), and we were in a different country. It snowed 20 inches the day the moving van arrived, and that set the pattern for the winter. I couldn't read any signs because they were all in French, the temperature would sometimes drop to -25 degrees Fahrenheit and the socialized medicine was substandard.

Despite these setbacks, I decided to embrace my new life with a can-do attitude. I enrolled my kids in English-speaking playgroups to meet other moms and to learn the ropes about everything from how to get a driver's license, to how to find good doctors and dentists.

Once I got the kids settled and found a babysitter for them, I decided to take French-immersion classes to learn about the culture and the language. To my surprise, a few months later (and after some wine), I found myself at a dinner party conversing fluently in French while my husband and his boss stood back amazed. I was so proud of myself and my achievement: Perseverance and determination had paid off. I actually took control of my circumstances and was able to converse. (Moreover, I could actually help my kids in school now.) This was a flash of the sort of character I'd need down the road.

My husband continued his corporate climb with a lot of late-night outings with clients, sometimes not returning home until 3 or 4 in the morning. I would wake up and panic that he was dead on the side of the road and call hospitals to see if he were registered. (In the late '80s, of course, we didn't have cellphones.) Then he would come in after a night of partying and say, "I didn't want to wake you." I was so infuriated that he didn't call, and because I was so angry, I couldn't fall back asleep. I finally told him just to stay downtown if he planned on being out late with certain clients. His days at the office grew longer and longer as he planned dinner engagements or just worked late. I became resentful about having to deal with the kids' problems and illnesses by myself, and my nagging, self-loathing and loneliness were not anything he wanted to come home to.

Weekends proved to be respites from these destructive patterns, because we did many family activities with other couples. My husband and I frequented downtown restaurants. We threw dinner parties where neighbors would bring dishes from their native countries. We'd ski or go tobogganing with the kids, or watch their school activities. He was an active participant in the family when he was present, and I loved the connection we had despite his drinking. He was a fun guy to be around.

After the death of my dad in 1992, my husband and I both wanted to be closer to our families. So in 1993 we moved to Bucks County, and my husband worked remotely, often traveling throughout North America and Canada. I found myself lonely again and, in an effort to combat that, trying to control the people, places and things around me. I became busy with volunteering at the children's school and immersing myself again in their activities. Keeping busy was my antidote. It meant I didn't have to think about how lonely I was, or how increasingly disconnected I felt from my husband who didn't want to discuss our changing relationship because it always ended in a confrontation.

After five years in Bucks County, we moved again to Mendham, New Jersey. Our children were entering middle and high school; and my husband was still traveling. When he did come home, his return was always heralded by drinking. Over time, his drinking escalated, and eventually the kids started to notice that dad was acting stupid. They were old enough at that time to realize that his behavior was not normal.

On the outside, it looked like I had it all: nice house, nice clothes, great vacations and two beautiful children. On the inside, however, I was dying. I had to admit that my perfect marriage was, in fact, not. My knight in shining armor was, in fact, a real person who had real problems. While my husband and I were at counseling, I found out that those problems were my problems, too — he had built up a mountain of lies between us. I felt like my world was crumbling around me, and so my inner-control freak leapt into action. I argued, nagged, controlled and tried to fix things. When that didn't work, my counselor told me to go to Al-Anon, which is based on the 12 Steps of Alcoholics Anonymous but meant for families and friends of those with substance-abuse problems.

This program was a tremendous help to me. It affects all areas of a person's life, and it helped me to create happy and fulfilling relationships with my mom and my children. By working in Al-Anon, and by undergoing psychotherapy with Eye Movement Desensitization and Reprocessing (EMDR), I gradually realized that the blame could not be placed entirely on my husband. I had a lot of codependency traits, like trying to control and fix things, feeling ashamed and living my life as a victim. I didn't realize that I was entitled to feel what I was feeling, because during my childhood and throughout my marriage, I was usually told that I was overreacting. I also didn't realize that the abandonment and shame I experienced in my childhood had become emotional triggers in my marriage and other relationships. Gradually, I came to recognize this about myself, and recognition is essentially the power to change.

And yet, that was not my happy ending.

In July 2005 we returned to Bucks County, Pennsylvania, and my husband lost his job after 20 years. He fought for a generous 19-month severance package and, with that in our back pocket, we invested heavily in a high-risk venture company where my husband had accepted a position. After one-and-a-half years, it went belly-up and we lost hundreds of thousands of dollars. My reaction? "Okay, we still have our house and our health. We will be all right."

That same year, my best friend died of breast cancer, my daughter had to take leave from Penn State due to personal issues and menopause hit me big time. I was crying constantly, and my husband said to me, "Honey, I want to invest more money into a franchise."

This was a unilateral decision — he was going to do it with or without my support. Which floored me after five moves, two children, years of counseling and even more years spent married to one another. Did he actually have the balls to do this?

But this turned out to be one piece of a much bigger puzzle. The new franchise, you see, was a religious company, and my husband felt a calling to be part of it. My husband, whom I had known and loved for so many years, had started reciting scripture and putting God first in his life. I saw glimpses of this fundamental religious conversion coming but never thought it would become a lifestyle. My husband was active in church as a child, and it was his faith that helped him get sober. While I hadn't been raised with the same level of church involvement, my own faith had become stronger during my time in Al-Anon: I had hit my emotional bottom so many times in my marriage, and that led me to rely heavily on God.

Still, my religious path was very different from that of my husband, and I certainly wasn't ready for the financial and emotional commitment this new faith suddenly required. (Especially since I had zero say in the matter.) As a result of my husband's decision, I thought my head was going to explode. "How could you," I demanded, "spend more money after we lost so much?" His reply? He saw it as making money in a down economy. In a way, he was vindicated: The company is doing well, thank goodness. But the catalyst that got us here, the action that triggered the change, was still fundamentally wrong. Never in our marriage had he made a major decision without me.

In hindsight, I recognize that he needed this: Finally, he was calling the shots in his career. But at the time I felt like a cue ball bouncing off one ball to the next. I wanted to be the cue stick! Yet I felt powerless over my destiny and my life; I was just reacting to circumstances. But then, as I was crying on the patio after a therapy session, furious that he had done this, I had an epiphany. Suddenly I realized that I did in fact have a choice. I had a choice! Wow! It never dawned on me that I could plan how I was going to live my life. I was always there for everybody, and then suddenly I realized it was my turn to take care of me.

But could I really go back to school at the age of 53?

There was a voice inside of me that said I needed to do more and help others, to pay it forward. This voice, I believe, was my soul telling me that helping others is what I am meant to do. So I stepped out of my comfort zone and started investigating schools and majors. After considering many different master's programs, I heard about life coaching, gave it a try and loved it. I registered that day. But it meant making a two-and-a-half-hour trip by train to New York City and taking a subway alone, which I had never done before. My passion, however, superseded my fear. I knew I could do this, and I was committed. The big question was how I would pay for it. We were still living off our savings, and funds were running low, but I had the support of my family, and I pressed on. Two weeks after registration, a refund check from an insurance company arrived in the mail — it was for the exact amount of the certification fee! I knew at that moment that this was my divine purpose in life, and today I still love it.

Over time, my mission has become to get the word out to women that we always have a choice. What's more, we must have confidence in trusting our choices. We are in control of our lives, successes, money and happiness. We just have to make the choice to leave victim-hood behind, face our fears and be courageous.

Reflections

How many times have you had a thought about something great...and then ignored it, because the idea of you doing it was just absurd? You had all these negative voices in your head telling you the countless ways you couldn't. Now think about what your life would be like if you could turn those voices off, trust your gut, move through the fear and simply do it? Where would you be now?

When making a choice — about a job, a relationship, a pet, whatever — your perspective is critical. Look at the potential change as a learning experience instead of viewing your current situation with anger, apathy or frustration.

Remember, you are always in control of your thoughts and actions. Clarifying your feelings — and figuring out a solution to a problem — requires you to create awareness around your thoughts.

Consider the following:

Are you listening to the negative talk in your head, or listening to the positive messages and acting on those instead? You are your thoughts. Replace negative talk with positive affirmations. Be aware of what you're thinking. Every time you say, "can't," or, "need," replace it with, "I choose," "I want," and, "I deserve."

Surround yourself with positive people (and steer clear of the negative people) in your life. Who can support you? What is the impact of surrounding yourself with positive, uplifting people? What kind of support can they provide as you progress toward your dream or vision? Who in your life must you spend less time with?

_____

_____

_____

_____

So now you want to pursue this dream. It's time to get the facts. Find somebody who does what you want to do, and use him/her as a mentor. Read, and talk to as many people as you can about it. Get the pros and the cons of your vision. You need to understand which adversities you'll have to overcome to make it happen. Anticipating the obstacles will help you persevere during those times when it seems almost impossible to move forward. Also, think about yeses and nos. Where must you say yes to make your dream happen? What choices must you make? Where must you say no? What must you stop doing?

_____

_____

_____

_____

Trust in yourself and a higher power, and follow your passion. What are the advantages of letting go and letting God take over? Less stress and anxiety? Being more open to things happening around you? Many times experiences unfold and fare better than you could ever imagine. Be tenacious, and you'll see doors open for you unexpectedly.

Acknowledgments

The process of writing and editing (and rewriting) a book is not a lonely business. One can't hide oneself away in an attic room somewhere with nothing but transcripts and the glow of a computer screen for company. At least I couldn't.

I'd like to extend, first and foremost, a big thank-you to the 11 bold and courageous women who joined me in sharing their stories, all with the hope that others could find the inspiration therein to change their own lives for the better.

I would also like to thank my family, my mother, my Mastermind groups and my coaches and mentors, Bill Kegg, Pamela Mattsson and Ron Renaud, all of whom believed in me and offered unfailing encouragement as I pursued this project.

My personal trainer, Sabrina Willard, deserves a round of applause as well for telling me about life coaching in the first place. Her tip set me on a career path that has challenged and fulfilled me in ways I could never have imagined.

Thank you to Wellington Photography for excellent photos. And, finally, a huge kudos is owed to Green Eye for Design, as the folks there creatively tackled the other big part of my book-writing project: the graphic design and layout. You make my words look better!

Sherry Shoemaker